Andrew Kennedy Hutchison Boyd

Counsel and Comfort

Spoken from a City Pulpit

Andrew Kennedy Hutchison Boyd

Counsel and Comfort
Spoken from a City Pulpit

ISBN/EAN: 9783744664370

Printed in Europe, USA, Canada, Australia, Japan

Cover: Foto ©ninafisch / pixelio.de

More available books at **www.hansebooks.com**

COUNSEL AND COMFORT

BY THE AUTHOR OF

"THE RECREATIONS OF A COUNTRY PARSON."

LONDON:
LONGMANS, GREEN, AND CO.
1868.

CONTENTS.

Contents.

COUNSEL AND COMFORT SPOKEN

FROM A CITY PULPIT

CONCERNING THE CLOSE OF HOLIDAY-TIME: WITH SOME THOUGHTS ON PULPITS.

COME, my friend, and let us walk backwards and forwards along this gravelled path, already beaten by my solitary feet for an hour past. It is not a carriage drive: but a path intended for saunterers on foot. It is broad enough for two: and the more especially if one of them, through the force of circumstances, chances to take up no space. And to-day you are at Constantinople; and I am here. I am not quite sure as to the precise number of miles between us; but there are many hundreds, I know.

You know this place well; and you would like this walk. On one hand, there is a level plot of closely-mown grass, of what may be esteemed considerable extent by a man of moderate ideas. And the prominent object on that side is a pretty Gothic house, built of red sandstone, set upon a green terrace. The house is backed by a wooded cliff: a cliff wooded from base to summit. For in every crevice of the rock trees have rooted themselves: that is, have been planted without man's help.   And the cliff looks like a warm bank of thick foliage, now crisp and russet. That cliff is ninety feet high : no very great height ; yet, let me say, rather higher than the rocks at the Land's End.   But on the other hand, there is our great sight.   On the other side of this little gravelled walk, which is a hundred and fifty yards in length, and nearly straight, let me tell you what there is. First, there is a border line of grass, the prettiest and least troublesome of all edgings for walks.   The well-defined outline of the grass and gravel makes a simple contrast of which one never tires.   Then there is a little boundary thicket made of pines of various sizes, also of laurels and yews : with here and there a staring sunflower. Beyond, there is a hedge of thorns, backed by a stone wall, five feet in height, which forms the boundary of this small domain.   And though on the farther side of the wall there is a narrow public road, the sea beyond it seems (when you look from this side) to wash the foot of that fortification.   You feel as though you were walking on a quarter-deck. In fact, the waves are lapping on the large stones within a dozen yards.   And so, backwards and for-wards along this gravelled path, is backwards and forwards by the shore of the great sea.

Yet this is not the boundless ocean, over which you look away and away, and think that America is on its other side.   This is but an arm of the Atlantic. It is the estuary of a river, not especially renowned in song. No poet has done for it what Burns did for the Doon by which he drew his first breath. **Here,** the estuary is four miles in breadth. On the farther side there is an island, rich in soil and genial in climate, where many worn-out sufferers have been able to breathe out in peace their last winter-time in this world. Its name was not a pleasing one to those English folk who hated an unpopular Scotch Prime Minister, many years ago. **And over that** island you may see **a line** of mountain-peaks which will bear being looked at though you may have come straight from Chamouni. Of course, they are not so high as Mont Blanc : and they have no solitudes of everlasting snow. Yet that is a glorious outline against the Western sky, at sunset or at midday : **and no** part of the height of those mountains is lost. **For** the height **of** mountains **is** reckoned **in** feet above **the** sea-level : **and here are** the sea-level and the mountain-tops together.

This **is** an autumn afternoon : one of the latest of September. And the fading woods suggest **to one's** mind a man with gray hair, wearing **down.** For the autumnal tint upon **our head is gray,** passing **into** white. **We do** not wither **in** glory, like **crimson** maples and glowing beeches in the October sun. **But to-day there is not the bright** crisp frosty sunshine touching declining Nature into pensive beauty : but the light is leaden, **and all** the **sky** is made up of clouds that come down very close upon the earth and sea. The sea is dark and gloomy : and **it** breaks upon the beach with a surgy murmur, as you might think it would upon untrodden shores.

Our holiday-time ends to-morrow : and then comes the long stretch of work again. It is pleasant work, but hard work : and you shrink a little from the first plunge into it. And you know the confused, over-driven feeling of the first days at the collar, with twenty things you would wish to do in the time in which it is possible to do ten. Holiday-time, I think, is something like life. We begin it, with vague antici-pations of great rest and enjoyment. We find it, in fact, much less enjoyable than we had expected. And at its end, though we may be conscious of a certain unwillingness to resume our load, we yet feel that our holiday-time is outworn ; and we are in some sort of way content to bid it good-bye. Yet it is a trial to say goodbye to anything : and in bidding farewell to times and places, we feel that we shall never have those things again quite the same. Even if there should come to none of us any of those great changes which hang over all human beings, there will be the sensible change, in fact and in feeling, that is ever advanc-ing upon all persons and all things here. Then when you are far away from your home and its duties, all these come to look somewhat misty and undefined. You forget those little ways which make up your habi-tude of being. And all future time is hidden by a cloud through which we strive in vain to see. You do not know where you are going : nor what trials may be sitting and waiting for you by the wayside, not far on. There is a great uncertainty, and an indefinite fear. You have had your troubles, some of them just as heavy as you could bear: and what life has been, it must be. And many minds know a good deal of the Roman Emperor's foreboding, that if things have long gone well with you, then something amiss is very likely to come. If we could but all rise to the happier argument from the Past to the Future of a certain ancient (and inspired) Poet; and really believe that " The Lord HATH BEEN mindful of us : He WILL bless us !" The more common way of judging certainly is, that since all has been so pleasant for many days or years, now a smash is due. But though this way of judging be common; and though, to a superficial glance, it seems to be confirmed by facts ; it would be very easy to shew that it is entirely wrong.

There is something enviable in the state of people who can go away from a place without caring : who can say goodbye to pleasant acquaintances without the least regret. Many human beings feel parting to be so painful, that they would rather miss the previous pleasure than encounter the trial which must come at last. You will think of the kind old Matthew, on that beautiful April morning of which Wordsworth has so sweetly sung. On that April morning he was not an old man : and turning aside from his task of fishing, he stopped awhile beside his little daughter's grave. And having thought there of her sweet voice and her

fair face, he turned to leave her earthly resting-place .
when he met, hard by, another little girl like what his
child would have been, so blooming and so happy.
It was a pure delight to look at her : but Matthew
thought how fragile a possession she would be, and he
remembered how bitterly he had suffered when his
own child died. "I looked at her, and looked again,
and did not wish her mine." Yes, what you never have,
you never can lose. And some grim self-contained old
bachelor, who has given no hostages to fortune, who
cares for nobody but himself, presents but a very small
surface on which fate can hit him hard.

My friend Smith told me recently, that he esteems
the necessity of saying goodbye as a serious drawback
from the pleasure of foreign travel : and that his purpose is, in future tours, to cultivate, when abroad, the
acquaintance of only the most disagreeable of his
countrymen and countrywomen. Then, he will experience no other feeling than one of relief when they
disappear from his view, never to return. Hitherto,
his experience has been as follows. You fall in with
pleasant people, going the same way with yourself.
You find that great part of the insular reserve has been
thawed out of the usually shy Briton. Gradually, you
fraternise : and for a good many days, those pleasant
folk and you journey on together. You think better
of mankind : you did not think there were so many
agreeable people in the world. Probably you are not
accustomed to see many such at Tollerporcorum.

But at length you must go on your separate ways, and you part : feeling it is not likely that you should meet again.   And to do all this six or seven times in two months is trying.

All this, it is obvious, has nothing to do with the subject of Pulpits.   Yet that subject was mainly in the writer's mind, when he began to walk up and down this gravelled path.   All this forenoon he has been busied in arranging the material which has been spoken, on various past Sundays, from a certain pulpit in which he feels a very deep interest.   A former volume of the like material has been so happy as to find a very great number of readers: and naturally enough, another volume of sermons preached from the same place has been thought of.   Thinking of that pulpit made him think of pulpits in general : and especially of yours, my friend, who have all this while been walking more or less consciously by my side.

Your pulpit is a very handsome one of carved oak, dark with age.   It stands out, clear of the chancel, in a certain great church.   The church is not Gothic ; but it is one of the best of Palladian churches : great in size, massive and real in the materials of which it is made : with its great pillars and its arched aisles.   I am not able to suppress an unsophisticated respect for an edifice on which its builders were content to spend several scores of thousands of pounds.   And all around that church, though it stands in the heart of the greatest of great cities, there spreads a solemn expanse, pleasant to see, where people of many generations have met together, in the long sleep of death. Above all, that church is suited with a congregation that fills it with attentive faces and sympathetic hearts: and fond as one may pardonably be of church architecture, the great thing about a church is the living congregation, after all. Then your predecessor in that pulpit wears lawn sleeves: and the average mind feels as though a certain dignity were cast around the pulpit whence the next step was to the episcopal throne.

The writer has various predecessors in his pulpit. None of them are bishops: none can by possibility become such: because they are clergymen of a Church in which those dignitaries are not. As for the pulpit, I do not know of what kind of wood it is made: though I have preached from it exactly three hundred and fifty times. Of this I am well assured, that it is not made of the wood it seems. The painter's skill has made it look like oak: which it unquestionably is not. I have heard, indeed, of church oak in this country being ingeniously painted in a bad imitation of itself. The pulpit is hung with a pretty deep drapery of crimson velvet, a little faded from the brightness of earlier days. And no wonder: for the writer is faded somewhat through the wear of years; and that velvet is older than himself.

But he would not exchange that faded velvet for many times what it cost when new : and though that pulpit is not Gothic, except in the unfriendly sense in which Sir Christopher Wren first applied the word, there is to him, as to very many of his fathers and brethren, no place on earth where he likes so much to be. We have a Scotticism of expression, common among the elder clergy, which always falls pleasantly on the ear. "Where are you to be on Sunday?" say to a good Scotch minister : and the answer will probably be, "AT HOME." *That* means, in his own pulpit. There is something very touching, when you hear an old man thus speak of the place whence he has spoken, on the most solemn of all subjects, to immortal beings committed to his care, through the Sundays of forty years. Yes : it is there, indeed, that we ought all of us to be most at home. I need say to none of my kindly readers, that I think a clergyman may very fitly write and speak upon subjects not directly theological or religious. He may very properly write an article for *Fraser:* and no one for whose opinion he cares a rush will find fault. But all these things are as recreation : what he writes for the pulpit is work. All these things are excursions, are as holiday rambles : but in the pulpit he is at home. His first and best thoughts go THERE. And often entered, with a nervous feeling, not to be reasoned away : never entered, without a solemn prayer for

God's help and blessing: the pulpit of every clergy-man whose heart is in his work is surrounded by memories and associations of such heart and happiness as are not to be expressed in words.

The pulpit (let the word be understood physically and morally) has been to the writer a matter of special interest from his earliest days. Very many are the pulpits in which he has stood. He does not mean for the purpose of preaching from them. But he cannot enter any church, great or small, on a day when it may be surveyed freely, without ascending the pulpit and looking at the church from that elevation. It may be said, for the information of such as have never entered any pulpit, that a church, viewed from that point, looks entirely different from what it looks, being viewed from any other. And as a general rule, the church looks a great deal larger.

Nothing brings out more strongly the difference in the tastes and likings of different men, than their feeling as to the pulpit. Some, a lesser class, feel an invincible gravitation towards the place: an extreme interest in all that concerns it. There are men, who, being far away from home, and going to a strange church on a Sunday, are aware of a longing almost like the thirsty wayfarer's for drink, to mount the pulpit and pour forth the message with which they are charged, to their fellow-sinners. As for the great majority of educated men, not to mention women, the pulpit is the very last place of which they ever think in relation to themselves. Not merely have they no desire to enter it: they have never even gone the length of asking themselves whether they would like to enter it or not. The whole thing appears quite out of the question. You and I, my reader, have probably never seriously considered whether we should like to be Prime Minister. And more: men who have chosen the Church for their profession; or rather who have been pushed gradually into orders without any conscious choice; having actually tried the pulpit, found it did not suit them: did not suit their tastes, even where it was conspicuously suited to their abilities: and so have made up their mind not to enter it any more. The writer has a very eminent and illustrious friend, who having preached three or four times, found or fancied that the pulpit did not suit him; and renounced it. Yet the pathetic eloquence which he has at command; and a charm of style which would constrain most people to listen in breathless attention to him discoursing upon any subject; would assuredly have made him one of the most interesting of all preachers. But the whole thing did not suit him: the proof being that he was content to give it up. The man who has in him the spirit and making of the preacher, could not be kept out of the pulpit. Not the railway and the locomotive have greater affinity one to the other, than that singular elevation and he. Men have been great and wise *there,* who were weak and foolish everywhere else. "He ought to be definitively confined to the pulpit, and fed over the side of it with brose and kirn-milk," said the homely Chalmers of a certain man who in the pulpit was a great orator, and out of the pulpit a great fool. And worldly inducements go for very little here, if the true nature of the preacher be inherent. You have heard of men who renounced fame and fortune, heartily and cheerfully, that they might devote strength and life to the sacred office: who made their choice, perhaps, with the enthusiasm of early youth; but never lived to regret it though they lived to fourscore.

The essential characteristic of the Pulpit is this: that it should be an elevated place in a church, whence the preacher may address the congregation. Let me, in passing, express the great disapproval with which I sometimes hear a Christian congregation spoken of as an *audience:* a *good audience* meaning a large congregation: a *bad audience*, or a *thin audience*, meaning a small congregation. There is, indeed, a lower deep than this: it is to speak of a *crowded house:* meaning a congregation which fills its church. Let not phrases taken from the theatre or the lecture-room be used concerning the house of God. But to resume. There are countries, as everybody knows, where the pulpit is essentially and exclusively associated with the sermon. There are others, and there is one in particular very well known to the writer, in whose National

Church prayers and sermon are spoken from the same place: and save at the celebration of the Holy Communion, the entire church service is performed from that spot. Yet even in that country, the name of the pulpit naturally suggests the sermon.

And what varieties there are of the thing! You have possibly seen pulpits of all degrees, from the huge erection piled up against a pillar in the nave of a great foreign cathedral: an erection which must dwarf the preacher, and which in fact is seldom used: down to the rickety box of deal stuck against the wall of a little Scotch country church; unpainted and undraped and worm-eaten. Even from such a pulpit has the writer not unfrequently preached: sometimes to country folk whose intelligent and hearty attention made one forget the unworthy edifice which was esteemed good enough for the worship of Almighty God. Once upon a time, in a certain rural parish, such was the writer's own pulpit: but of course *that* would not do: and a little representation in the right quarter soon made it give place to decorous dark oak and crimson. Let me say, that I cannot understand those clergymen who do not care a whit how shabby their church may be: and who contrive, as I have witnessed, to provide the parish with a most elegant and comfortable parsonage, leaving the poor old church a mortifying contrast of dirt and squalor. Then there are pulpits of wood and of stone: the latter sometimes of one block of freestone.

gracefully carved over its surface, like that beautiful pulpit in the cathedral of Chester: sometimes of marble, a costly piece of inlaid work, like that elaborate pulpit at All Saints in London: sometimes resting on a clustered shaft of porphyry or granite, and displaying panels enriched with figures in high relief, like that most pleasing pulpit at St Anne's in Dublin. Sometimes those stone pulpits are warmly padded inside with crimson cloth: sometimes they are cold white marble within, unrelieved by a vestige of drapery, very chilling to look at, and (one would say) to preach from. Sometimes pulpits are very high; sometimes ostentatiously low: in the latter case in churches in England where the childish idea has been admitted, that to make the pulpit loftier than the reading-desk is to " elevate the place of preaching above the place of prayer." Sometimes the pulpit proper is lost in a huge erection of stairs and terraces and platforms and ugly iron railings, filling up the end of a church in which there is no altar: as though to announce to all comers, Here the sermon is the first thing. Sometimes it is a little projecting jug of stone, in a modest corner, as though to say, Here the sermon is no great matter. And to say the truth, in such cases it generally is no great matter. I could easily name a church where I have been present at a choral service, performed by forty surpliced choristers with admirable taste and skill: and where the sermon which followed, though short, was extremely tedious;

and in fact was so bad that it could not by possibility have been worse. Sometimes you may find a stone pulpit in the open air, as that at Magdalen College at Oxford, whence the University sermons were sometimes preached. There is in England a parish church where the pulpit consists of a velvet-covered easy chair, with a music stand placed in front of it. The builders of that church are recorded to have resolved to erect a church which no human being, on a cursory inspection, would take to be a church ; and they have to a great degree succeeded in their intelligent purpose. We have all heard of " Henley's gilt tub," whence that fluent mountebank gave his celebrated lecture on the way to make a pair of shoes in five minutes. A great crowd of shoemakers assembled, drawn by the announcement of a discourse which would have been to them of such practical value : but the shoemakers were conscious that they had been deluded, when the orator produced a pair of boots, and in five minutes cut off their tops and left them shoes. There have been preachers who eschewed the pulpit, preferring a large stage on which they might strut to and fro. The writer has never seen any of these ; and never will see any of them. There is a vile custom, which originated in America, but which has been introduced into several places of worship in this country, of substituting for the pulpit a considerable platform, provided with a sofa, and having a counter in front behind which the preacher stands. An English traveller, having entered a large building in the United States, perceived such an erection at one end of it. A great congregation had assembled. In a little, a human being, with a hat on his head and a greatcoat on his back, walked up the centre passage. Stopping at the foot of the stair, he got out of his great-coat and took off his hat: and then, ascending the platform, appeared to be the individual who was to conduct the service. Some people, no doubt, think all this simple and unaffected. Some people would doubtless agree with the writer in esteeming it irreverent and disgusting in a very high degree. Yet let me recall a horrid Scotch custom, seen in my youth, of the officiating clergyman hanging up his hat on a peg beneath the sounding-board of the pulpit, to remain there till the service was over. For a bishop, or a preacher in a cathedral, to lay his cap on the cushion before him, is all very well: but a hat, not unfrequently a very bad one, hung on a peg, can never look seemly or decorous. There is a reprehensible and offensive taste for the tawdry in the matter of pulpit decoration, in several quarters in Scotland. In some instances this might be justified by the consideration, that the pulpit is thus brought into harmony with the discourse which is delivered from it. I have beheld a pulpit of white and gold: another painted light green: another which was of a roseate hue. If people cannot see how unbecoming that kind of thing is, it is quite useless to try to shew them. The right pulpit, in ordinary cases, and

where expense is a consideration, is doubtless a plain
hexagonal or octagonal pulpit of oak. Let its colour
be always dark ; and its drapery always crimson. Let
the stair be not obtrusive. As a general rule, let there
be a sounding-board. It is usually of no use : but
there is a fitness in its aspect : and it helps to make
the pulpit, as it ought to be, utterly unlike any erection for any secular purpose. You should feel, as you
look at the thing, that it is a place which renders
essential a certain quietude and restraint of matter and
manner in all that may be said from it. I have heard
a very eminent preacher say, that you may fitly give
your sermon with all the energy you can display without lifting a hand; but that any gesticulation appeared
to him unsuited to the pulpit. I do not agree with
him ; though I believe his rule tends to the better and
safer extreme. And let me say that even the utmost
dulness appears preferable to the outrageous claptrap
which one sometimes hears reported. All jocular
matter is of course inadmissible : all bitter and sarcas-
tic remarks are unutterably offensive. I lately read in
a country newspaper an account of a discourse given
upon some occasion by a certain preacher. In that
discourse, the country newspaper said, the preacher
" shewed himself a master of wit and sarcasm." Without having heard the man, one can imagine the hateful exhibition. Controversial statements, too, are to be
avoided. The things spoken from the pulpit should
be those as to which the whole congregation is, at

least in speculation, agreed. It is inexpedient that the preacher should make strong statements which half his hearers will esteem to be absurd and false. And if such statements be wrong in the sermon, much more are they in the prayers. I have heard of an eminent Scotch divine who in his prayer before sermon begged the Almighty "to remit the judgments which might well be sent upon this country on account of that legislative measure most improperly called the Reform Bill." Such a petition enables one the better to understand the unconscious truthfulness of a statement lately published in an American journal. That journal declared, in all good faith, that the prayer offered by the Rev. Mr Smith on a certain occasion, was "the most eloquent prayer ever addressed TO A BOSTON AUDIENCE."

As for the matter spoken from the pulpit, I do not hesitate to say that if it be simple, earnest, and unaffected, it ought, as a general rule, to be exempted from all criticism. I speak, of course, not of published discourses: but of those which are preached in the ordinary course of duty. A clever writer in a literary paper lately maintained that it would waken up the members of a comatose profession, if the preaching of a sermon were held to be its publication; and if thereupon it might be subjected to the like unceremonious treatment with other published literary productions. That clever writer said that good would follow if we were occasionally to read in some

critical journal an article which should begin by saying that "last Sunday the Rev. Mr Log ascended his
pulpit, and preached in his usual dull and stupid
fashion :" and if the article then proceeded to shew
in detail the badness of Mr Log's reasoning, the in-
felicity of his illustrations, and his general unfitness
to instruct his fellow-men. I venture to differ from
the clever writer already spoken of. It is conceivable
that the homely discourse, though it did not please a
sharp critic going to hear the preacher for one day,
might yet do good to the people for whom it was written : who went to be instructed rather than to criticise;
and who knew by long experience the faithfulness and
diligence of the good man who preached it. Religious instruction need not be brilliant, nor eloquent,
nor original, to serve very effectually the great end at
which all worthy religious instruction aims. And that
end, it may be said, is not to satisfy a chance reviewer
who has dropped into church by accident : but to
benefit and comfort the congregation which habitually
worships there.

Yet it may be recorded for the gratification of such
as may differ from me, that there are localities in
which a system is carried out which subjects religious
instruction to a severe censorship. I recently read the
advertisement of an enterprising bookseller, which
said, that with the view of inducing children to take
more interest in going to church, the bookseller had
prepared a series of printed schedules, which might be

purchased in a form like that of a bank cheque-book. On each Sunday morning the child might be supplied with a schedule torn out of this book, and with a pencil. And while in church, the child might note down upon blank spaces provided, the preacher's name: his text: the way in which he handled his subject: and some appreciation of his voice and manner; whether good, bad, or indifferent. A friend of mine saw one such schedule, after it had been filled up by a boy of ten years old. Under the head of *Manner*, the youthful critic had written the words, MIGHT BE IMPROVED. Probably the province of criticism could hardly be extended farther. You can imagine how much likelihood there is that a child trained to go to church in such a spirit, would ever be impressed or improved by sermons listened to for the purpose of passing judgment upon them. And you can imagine how that child, having grown up, would develop into the human being who would employ that unutterably hateful expression which people in America employ when they desire to praise their preacher: the expression, to wit, that he is *a preacher who* GIVES SATISFACTION.

So let us turn away from the leaden sky and the sullen waves. They will be oftentimes blue and bright before we see them again.

II.

THANKFULNESS.

"Be ye thankful."—Col. iii. 15.

THERE is a picturesque tract of the Western Highlands of Scotland, in passing through which the traveller has to ascend a long, winding path, very steep, very rough, and very lonely, leading up a wild and desolate glen. The savage and awful grandeur of the scenery, with its bare hills and rocks, is hardly equalled in this country. But if the traveller goes up that glen on foot (and it is hardly possible to go up it otherwise), his appreciation of the scene around him is gradually overborne by the sense of pure physical fatigue. Not without a great strain upon limbs and heart, can that rugged way be traversed. At last you reach a ridge, whence the road descends steeply on the other side of the hill. You have ended your climbing, and you may now begin to go down again, from whichever side you come. And there, at this summit, you will find a rude seat of stone, which bears the inscription in deeply-cut letters, REST AND BE THANKFUL. Many weary travellers have rested there : let us trust that a good many have been thankful.

We all know that the like name has been given to more than one or two like resting-places : that it is borne by various seats, at the top of various steep ascents in this country. There is something pleasing, and something touching, in the simple natural piety which has dictated the homely name. He was a heathen who said it, but he spoke well who said, Wheresoever man feels himself in peace and rest, let him think of God, and give thanks to Him. I have no doubt at all, that St Paul would have heartily approved that inscription in Glencroe : and would have felt that there is something to warm the heart, when the solitary traveller finds in that lonely place, without a human dwelling or a human being near, the brief reminder of the presence and the goodness of Him who is present as much in the wild waste as in the peopled city ; and from whose mercy all our blessings come, whether small or great : from the few minutes' breathing-space in the Highland glen, up to the last unspeakable gift of His Son to die for us, and His Blessed Spirit to sanctify and console. For you see the comprehensive duty, which is enjoined in the few words of the text. The great Apostle would impress upon those Christians of Colosse, who have ceased from their work and warfare through so many centuries now, how many things those should seek to do, who trust they are "risen with Christ." There is a long list of Christian duties in this chapter in which the text stands. There is sketched out a character and a life which, if manifested and led by all who bear the Christian name, would make this world a very holy and a very happy place. St Paul tells the Colossians how they ought to "set their affection on things above:" how they ought to mortify the evil impulses of a fallen, though renewed nature: putting off anger, malice, falsehood, and every evil word and deed, and putting on the new man, in which God's holy image is restored. He bids them put on, as becomes the elect of God, mercy, kindness, humility, meekness, long-suffering: he bids them forbear and forgive, even as the kind Redeemer forgave: he bids them put on charity, as a robe that should take in every Christian virtue and grace: and he bids them let God's peace rule in their hearts. And then, like a link in this golden chain, like a cope-stone on this beautiful structure, comes the short text with its wide and large meaning: which tells us of one pervading principle and affection which should leaven the believer's whole heart and life : which reminds us how there should go with him, everywhere, the deep sense that there is an unseen hand that gives him all he receives: the deep sense that he is a weak, dependent, undeserving creature, meriting so little, and receiving so much: "loaded with benefits," "prevented with the blessings of God's goodness:" remembered with "compassions that fail not," but are "new every morning:" even afflicted, when afflicted at all, unwillingly, and in faithfulness and love. Remember all these other duties, the great Apostle seems to say: but never forget *this;* "Be ye thankful!"

We have heard of things and people being conspicuous by their absence. And I think you will feel, my friends, that there is a certain Name, which is not mentioned in my text, which by its omission is only the more solemnly and impressively suggested to us. Yes, the meaning which is hinted, which is suggested and implied but not expressed, is sometimes for *that* only the more effectually conveyed. And as with the inscription on the stone seat, so with the precept which forms my text: there is something very striking in what is omitted, as well as in what is said. "Rest and be thankful," says the stone in the Highland glen: "Be ye thankful," says St Paul to the Christians of Colosse. It is not said to *whom* we are to be thankful. There is a touch of natural piety in the fact, that *that* does not need to be said. *That* is taken for granted! We all know Who it is that is the Giver of ALL good: and when we are told, generally, to be thankful, of course we know to Whom! Resting at the summit of the mountain path, it is not to the man who erected that seat for the weary traveller: though it is fit and right that he should be kindly thought of while we are enjoying the effect of his work, yet we are to look beyond *him* to a cause above him. *He* erected that seat, acting (as it were) for God: every mortal who

does a kind and good deed, in a right spirit, is acting
for God, and in God's name : and he went away when
his work was done, asking of the wayfarer, putting his
request on record with a pen of iron upon the stone,
—that for whatever comfort and rest might be experienced there, the wayfarer might bestow his thanks in
the right quarter.   And St Paul does just the same !
Hundreds and hundreds of years since, just the same !
He says no more than this, " Be ye thankful :" as one
who felt that those he addressed would know, as well
as himself, what is the kind Hand from which *all*
blessings flow !

" I am very thankful," says the poor invalid, who
amid great suffering is permitted a little blink of ease.
" I can never be thankful enough," the parent says,
when told that his little child has weathered the worst,
that the crisis of disease is past, and that the little
thing is to be spared.   " Oh for a more thankful
heart," the Christian has many a time said, going out
from church on a communion Sabbath, when the
Saviour has been very plainly present at His table,
and the Blessed Holy Spirit has breathed warmly
upon the heart, and when some little of Christ's love,
and Christ's peace, has been felt and known.   You
do not ask such people to whom they are thankful !
Oh, there is but One !   One, who is the Giver of *every*
good gift : and to Whom all gratitude tends at the
last.   There may be steps, as it were, on the way up
to Him : kind human friends, and happy second

causes : but it all comes to Him in the end.   If the kindly medicine did it : if the bracing breeze did it : if the cheerful, hopeful word from a loving heart did it : oh, it was God that did it all !   Yes, all gratitude runs up to Him : to Him as manifested in our Blessed Saviour's face.   No need for the rough seat amid the heather, to say, " Rest, and be thankful *to God:*" no need for St Paul to tell us, " Be ye thankful *to God.*" We all know *that.*   There is none good but One. There is one Giver of *all* good !

There are indeed many places where St Paul speaks out his meaning fully : tells it all in so many words. " Thanks be unto God," he says, " for His unspeakable gift."   " Thanks be unto God, who giveth us the victory, through our Lord Jesus Christ."   And cheered in an anxious time by the sight of Christian friends, Paul " thanked God, and took courage."   And you all know how there runs through the great Apostle's writings a strain as to the great duty of thankfulness. You remember how, speaking of the heathen world, he tells that its condemnation was that, " when they knew God, they glorified Him not as God, neither were thankful."   And you remember, too, that strong counsel to the saints at Ephesus, " Giving thanks always for all things unto God and the Father in the name of our Lord Jesus Christ."

Here, then, is the mood of spirit in which the true Christian should be seeking to go on through life.   " Be ye thankful."   Every one here knows **well**, how great a part of Christian duty, of **vital** religion, consists in the cultivation of spiritual states, not outwardly seen : of conditions of temper, affection, will, and judgment, which make but a small **and** imperfect manifestation of themselves in external **deeds.** There **are** many such graces which we ought **to** be daily cultivating : praying for those influences **of** the Blessed Spirit which are to the graces of the soul as the gentle summer rain and the warm summer sunshine to green grass and green leaves. But we may be sure that there is none that is more weightily incumbent upon us, none from whose faithful cultivation we shall in many ways get more good, than this great fundamental and all-pervading grace of gratitude towards God. **It** *is* a happy temper to come to, and **one that is** worth some pains and thought to reach, that whenever we are enjoying anything good, any blessing that has come,—when things go as we would wish, when some trouble or anxiety has been removed, **—we** should think, Now I know from Whom all this comes,—and be thankful to Him. It is a great addition to the value of any happy thing that comes to us, **if we** train ourselves to this : not to thank our stars, **or think how** lucky we have been : but to take it all **as proof of a** kind God's remembrance, of His love or His forbearance and patience.

Now, **it** may be replied to all this, No doubt *that* is a most happy temper to come to : no doubt, there is hardly a thing which can come a numan being's way, for which he should be more thankful, than for a thankful heart. But then, is *that* a thing that can be got, if nature or grace has not given it to you? There are people of that happy, hopeful, cheerful, contented, humble, trusting disposition, that they always look at the bright side of things: they really have a great deal to be thankful for: and they are able to see it. Other people, again, are naturally anxious; desponding: they cannot help looking on to the future with a certain vague fear: and they have a very heavy burden of anxiety and care actually resting on them. They really have not so much to be thankful for: and though they honestly desire to think of God's kindness and their own ill-deserving, still " care's unthankful gloom" has settled down upon them: and they are not able to be thankful: that is, to have thankfulness as the prevailing and habitual temper of their heart and mind: it is not *in* them to have *that:* and one of the saddest things about their sad lot, that this should be so.

I will confess that there is a certain measure of truth in all this. You cannot determine that your heart shall be thankful, just as you might determine that your hands shall be clean. It is not so directly and completely under the control of your will, as *that.* I believe there may be Christian men and women, daily confessing before God with tears their unthankfulness and lack of trust in Him: daily praying earnestly for more thankfulness, and more faith that

" The Lord will provide." And yet, when St Paul in the text says to you and me, my friends, " Be ye thankful," there is implied in that command, that this is a thing so far under control that it may fitly be commanded. It is thus far under our own control: that by God's grace we may attain it if we honestly try. And you know there is no Christian grace we can attain on any other terms. There is no Christian duty we can do, unless by that same help, God's grace and Spirit, freely offered. And your own common sense tells you, and your own observation of those around you tells you, that no doubt there *is* such a thing as fostering a querulous, discontented, unthankful spirit; and there *is* such a thing as culti-vating a humble, trusting, thankful one. To a certain degree, all this is under the control of the will. To a certain and great degree, people have this in their own hands. You have found it so yourselves. You know there are men and women who keep thinking mainly of the few things they would like which God has denied them; and who never think at all of the innumerable things they need, which God has given them, and continues to give them day by day; often while these blessings are never remarked, and habit-ually while the gift is received without the faintest breath of thankfulness to the great Giver. There are people who do all this constantly: whose whole life and talk is one long, ungrateful grumble: who seem to think that Almighty God has some grudge or spite against them : and all this, while they are incomparably more favoured by Him than is the vast majority of the race ; than are countless millions of immortal beings who deserve at God's hands exactly as much. Indeed, I doubt not you have sometimes thought, that as regards worldly aims and successes and advantages, it is often those to whom God has given most, who are least thankful to Him : it is often those who have already received worldly blessings by scores and hundreds, who keep up a constant querulous moaning if they are not suffered to get some one thing more : as if the fact that you have already got a vast deal, gave you a right to demand everything. And, not to think of others, has not each of you sometimes set your heart on something or other : and because God would not give you *that*, talked and felt as if you were released from all obligation to be grateful to God at all : forgot entirely the thousand things He daily gives you, in the bitter thought of the one thing He saw meet to deny? Now, by giving in to this, which doubtless is a tendency in fallen human nature,—by this brooding over the thing denied, and turning your back on the manifold things given,—you are just training yourselves to ingratitude towards God : you are sowing and watering and fostering that evil weed in your heart! You are flying in the face of this wise and kindly precept which makes the text. Oh how much better,—how much worthier and happier,—yea how much wiser,—to turn the other page :

to look how much you get, to think how little you deserve : to remember that you are a poor guilty sinner deserving only God's wrath and woe : to remember that you ought to be thankful that you are spared in the place of hope,—that you are out of perdition : to remember that every blessing that comes to you, comes simply and entirely of God's free grace and for Christ's sake : till in shame that such a creature as you should dare to be unthankful, should not be thankful to take the crumbs that fall from the Master's table, you fall on your knees, and hide your face, and pray for pardon for that ungrateful, murmuring, wicked spirit, to which you have been giving harbour !

I have remarked, brethren, and I am sure many of you have done the same,—that people who have received least at God's hand,—least, that is, in the way of earthly blessing,—are oftentimes the most thankful. I have seen the poor sufferer, more thankful to God for an hour of ease, than many a one of us is for a life in which we hardly ever know pain. I have known the bare dwelling of poverty, where a thankfulness that was painful to see, followed the little aid that might procure what was literally the " daily bread," for the poor, white-faced little hungry children : a thankfulness greater a hundred times than ever was expressed in the formal "returning of thanks" after a sumptuous feast ;—a giving of thanks so perfunctory and so heartless that one sometimes wonders how much real gratitude it is meant to

express ; or whether it is meant to express any at all.
Ay, there is more true thankfulness, more of the
recognition of a providing God, in that touching
picture you may have lately seen, of the poor old
fisherwoman and her little grand-daughter asking
God's blessing upon their sorry meal, than many of
us have many a time shewn with more reason to be
thankful : Oh my friends, there is a lesson and a
rebuke there for you and me ! Yes : I am not afraid
that from the most suffering, the humblest, the poor-
est, the objection will come to St Paul's precept in
the text, that truly they have very little to be thankful
for : not from bereaved hearts, not from crushed
hearts, not from beds of suffering and houses of death
will *that* undutiful objection come. My friends, I have
heard many a poor creature say, in the midst of suffering, privations, trials, the like of which you never
knew, "Oh, I have much to be thankful for !" And
you looked round the bare room, and you thought of
the comfortless lot ; you saw the aged, trembling hands,
and you heard the failing breath : and you thought how
such as walk by sight and not by faith, would have
wondered what it was that *that* poor creature had to
be thankful for. Yet you blest God in your heart,
that the solemn words were true! Yes, that sufferer
had much, yea very much to be thankful for ! No
earthly comfort, no worldly wealth, no human friends,
were worth *that* possession in the failing heart, which
had its solemn witness in that grateful spirit ! That

sufferer had "won Christ:" in the poor chamber His presence was truly felt: that sufferer had reached the strong consolation, the sanctifying grace, of God's Holy Spirit: that sufferer was going home to Heaven, to enter on the inheritance of martyrs and saints, and to rest in the rest of God! Ah, brethren, if ever true words were spoken on this earth, it was when the dying Christian said, He had much to be thankful for!

But we have been led into this train of thought, while remarking that thankfulness in the heart is a grace which may be cultivated, and that an ungrateful heart is a bad thing which may be put down: and that it depends a great deal more upon our own nature, and our own endeavours, aided by God's Spirit, whether we shall be thankful or not, than it depends upon our outward blessings and advantages. It is just those people who have fewest of these, that are many a time the most thankful. And every one can understand, that if the denial of worldly prosperity, and the sending of worldly trials and disappointments, be used by God, and sanctified by the Blessed Spirit, to make our souls prosper and be in health,—to lead us to Christ, and to make us choose Him for our eternal portion,—then there never was anything for which we had so good reason to be thankful, as for these dealings of God with us, painful as at the time they might be. You remember how the good and wise man Jabez, in old days, knew that God might "bless indeed," when mere worldly men might have fancied that He did not bless at all.　And if we have committed our souls to Christ, then, however hard it may oftentimes be to believe it, God will be blessing us by all He sends: " all things will work together" for our good : and we shall have good reason, like St Paul, to "give thanks always for all things." "Though He slay me, yet will I trust in Him," is the earnest purpose of the faithful spirit : and who can forget that noble example of steady faith in God's love through the darkest days,—the example of him who, when flocks and herds and children and all were reft from him on one black day, "fell down upon the ground and worshipped :" saying, "Naked came I out of my mother's womb, and naked shall I return thither : The Lord gave, and the Lord hath taken away ; blessed be the name of the Lord !"

And in all this, my friends, we have reached the true secret of thankfulness.　Only to true believers in Jesus, is this text, in its fullest and deepest sense, addressed : only by them can it be obeyed.　The mere worldly man may be grateful to the God of Providence, when all things prosper with him : when there is abundant reason for thankfulness, manifest to the eye of sense : but it is the true believer's unspeakable, inestimable privilege, to thank God for all.　"Be careful for *nothing;* but in *everything*, by prayer and supplication, with *thanksgiving*, let your requests be made known unto God :" and then "the peace of God, which passeth all understanding, shall keep

your hearts and minds through Christ Jesus." **To
"be thankful,"** as the text commands, is the especial
grace of the true believer: **of** him who *knows* that
God loves **him;** who sees in Christ's life and death
that God **loves him: and who is not to be shaken
from** that firm belief by the darkest, saddest, **most
perplexing** things that come. " I know my God too
well," the Christian says, " in a multitude of ways, to
be driven from my assurance **of** His love for me, **and
to be** driven from my gratitude to Him, even by trials
and sorrows He may send **me,** and whose purpose I
cannot in the least explain." " I really do not know,"
may be the believer's words, " why it has pleased God
to send me this long season of broken health : or why
He has set me in the last place in life I would have
chosen : or why He has denied me a blessing which **I
think no one would ever have enjoyed so much as
me : I really** cannot **explain** all *that :* but I know that
all God's dealings **with** me are kind and right: and
so by His Spirit's help I will thank Him **for it all !"**
Here, my friends, is the secret of thankfulness. Here
is the way in which **to** obey this great precept **of the
great Apostle Paul.** It has grown upon me, this **conviction, as I wrote** this sermon : and because **I am
sure of its solemn truth and** importance, I pray **that**
the **Blessed** Spirit **may impress it on all.** I had not
intended this treatment **of** my text : I had not intended
this line of thought at all. I had thought of a long
catalogue of blessings which God has freely given us :

things we all have for which to be thankful: and at another time I may fitly suggest these to you: but it is borne in upon me that *that* is not the way to waken and kindle real thankfulness in our hearts. True it is, indeed, that there is so very much that we have all freely received. True it is, that there is so very much we all get from God, and get for nothing. True it is, that there is a host of things which God must do for each of us every day, or we could not live: and true it is, above all, that God so loved us, that He sent His Son to die. All these truths we may well remember: and seek to grow more grateful to the great Benefactor when we " forget not all His benefits :" but beyond all this, is the training of our hearts to thankfulness: the putting down the hard and suspicious thoughts of God which will come when His benefits seem few and our anxieties many: the firm belief in His love for us; the steady faith that the darkest things are what we need, to train us for a better world. O brethren, if you would be truly thankful, seek an assured part in Christ till you get it; seek with your whole heart that the Holy Spirit may kill out in you all evil feelings and thoughts and affections,—may shew us what sinful creatures we are, undeserving the least of God's mercies,—may make our hearts glow with gratitude to Him who died for us, loved us, saved us! And if *that* be done, how little all other things will be! Reading back the story of our past lives, we shall see how wonderfully we have been led and kept at a hundred times and ways; till like the Psalmist, we say, "Bless the Lord, O my soul!" But if we have been of a surety led to Christ, then *that* sufficeth us. "Thanks be unto God," will be the utterance of our heart, "for His unspeakable gift," which includes or makes up for every other! "Unto Him that loved us, and washed us from our sins in His own blood, and hath made us kings and priests unto God and His Father; to Him be glory and dominion for ever and ever, Amen!"

And this thankful spirit, to which we may thus train ourselves in this life, by the guidance of the Holy Ghost, is one that will last with us for ever. Yes, it is fit and right, that through eternity, the songs of the redeemed should be songs of praise and thankfulness. Looking back, there, on the way by which they have been brought,—its temptations, perils, and sorrows: looking round on the glory and rest in which they are, and safe for ever to be: calling to mind the work and death of that Blessed One to whom they owe it all: what wonder if the spirit of adoring gratitude should be breathed through all the utterances of that great multitude, that shall stand before the throne, and before the Lamb! What wonder if their words shall be, "Blessing, and glory, and wisdom, and thanksgiving, and honour, and power, and might, be unto our God for ever and ever!" *There*, shall be thanksgiving consummate! "Blessing, and honour, and glory, and power, be unto Him that sitteth upon the throne, and unto the Lamb for ever!" Yes; *there*, at last, perfect thankfulness, and perfect rest. It is meet and well that to-day, in deep Glencroe, or amid green corn-fields and summer trees nearer hand, the wayfarer should sit down and thank God for that little blink of rest. But oh, in that Happy Place, where the believer is safe for ever; looking back upon earthly pain and sorrow, in the perfect peace of God: where no anxiety or care can ever come; where nothing shall distract or weary any more: where the believer shall have entered upon that Rest that remaineth for the people of God: and where the holy heart, wherein all sin is dead, shall yield no affection that is not pure as God is pure: then, my friends, in a glorious and sublime truth of sense, the pilgrim shall REST AND BE THANKFUL!

June 21, 1863.

III.

THE BLESSED COMFORTER.

"The Comforter, which is the Holy Ghost"—JOHN xiv. 26.

I SOMETIMES think, my friends, that there is One Person in the Godhead, whom we practically do somewhat slight. We do not think of Him so kindly and hopefully as we ought: we do not enough recognise Him as God, with the Father and the Son together to be worshipped and glorified. We seldom hear even a sentence in a prayer, addressed expressly to the Blessed and Holy Spirit, the Third Person in the Godhead. I do not believe that any among us doubts that there is such a Being: we are fully persuaded of His Personality, and His Agency, and the inestimable value and importance of the Work He does. We believe all that: May God help our unbelief and increase our faith! Yet still, I think we greatly fail practically to realise these things: We are ready to think of the Holy Ghost rather as an influence, an energy proceeding from God, than as a real kindly Person, loving us, caring for us, dwelling in us if that be God's gracious will. And yet, if we think at all, we cannot but feel that none can be more interested in our salvation : that none is more closely and completely linked with our whole Christian life : that there is none whose presence is so needful for us while we remain in this present evil world.

We can see a kind of reason for this lack of full and express recognition of the Blessed Spirit. No doubt,—no doubt, there is One Person in the Godhead, whom we love, and may fitly love, most of all. There is One, whose name (let us pray) will never fail to warm our heart, till our heart turns cold with the last chill it is to know. It is, doubtless, that beloved Redeemer who died for us: that Divine Person who took upon Himself our human nature ; and became our Elder Brother in humanity: that Blessed Saviour Jesus Christ, who went about doing good, and to whom little children came so naturally, drawn by the sweetness of that kind face and that gentle voice ; and concerning whom we seem to feel that, the Mighty God as He was, we could have gone to Him, and told our story to Him, rather in love and confidence than in fear.

It is not wonderful, brethren, that in the believing heart, Christ should always be the First ; yea, the All in All. And there is more and deeper in this than the mere weak impulse of our fallen nature. For in the face of Christ we see the glory of the whole Godhead. He is the Image of the Invisible God, Father, Son, and Spirit. And looking at Him, and loving

Him, we look at God, and we love God. And the visible representative, is, naturally, more conspicuous, more manifest, to our view, than the invisible Godhead which He represents. But, besides this right reason for special love to the Saviour, our Elder Brother, there is another wrong reason in many minds: a reason founding upon a notion which cannot be too carefully dispelled from your minds. This is the notion, entertained by many, that Christ is far kinder and milder and more easily won, than God the Father and God the Spirit: that God the Father, especially, is a stern, severe being, who would willingly have consigned us to all perdition: and that the gentler, kinder Son, interposed, and suffered, and saved us, almost against the angry Father's will. Oh, what a miserably false and unchristian way *that* is of regarding God! Is that the kind of idea conveyed to us by Christ, when He tells us that God waits to welcome back the sinner as kindly as the father did his prodigal son: and when He tells that the kindest-hearted among you is not so ready to shew kindness to your children, as He is to give every blessing to you! Always remember, brethren; and pray for grace to feel it far more really than you have ever yet done: that just what Christ was, God is: that when you desire to think of the Almighty Being above us, your right course is not to put your mind upon the stretch, to reach out to thoughts of infinite space and infinite years; but rather to open the Gospel of St Luke or St John, and to see Jesus of Nazareth as He trod this world; to listen to His comfortable words, to mark His deeds of mercy: to think of His never-failing compassion to the sorrowful, of His willingness to receive the sinful: to look on His unspeakable love to lost man, shewn in His life and His death: and then to remember that this same Jesus of Nazareth "hath shewn us the Father;" and that He is the "Image of the Invisible God!"

It is an end, my friends, to which a Christian minister can never devote too much care and thought, to dispel from the minds of the people committed to his ministry, the wrong ideas and beliefs which are so ready to creep in and establish themselves, as to Almighty God: as to His nature and character: as to how He feels towards us. And I cannot but frankly confess, that I believe there is no small measure of truth,—though truth stated in a most morbid and exaggerated fashion,—in what has been written by an eminent historian whose life and work were lately and sadly cut short together, as to the stern and gloomy views of our Heavenly Father entertained by not a few in Scotland. My desire and prayer at this time are, that we may this day be enabled rightly and truly to think of One who is indeed God : of One who cares for us as warmly and sincerely as the Redeemer Himself; of One who "makes intercession for us with groanings that cannot be uttered;" of One, to be worshipped and glorified as God; and to be loved and confided in only less than Him who died for us on the tree.

Let us remember, then, **that** in the Godhead, besides the Father and the Son, there **is a** Third Person : the same in substance, equal in power and glory : who is called the Holy Ghost, or the Holy Spirit : mysterious in His nature and being : proceeding from the Father and the Son : who spake by the prophets : **and who** fulfils certain great works in that wonderful operation which brings man from death to life ; and which makes man fit to dwell in God's beatific presence. We shall hereafter think of the varied operation of this Blessed Spirit : but let us now **think of** that one precious truth which our Saviour sets before us in the words of the text. See how our Lord names **Him** : "The Comforter, which is the Holy Ghost." And in several other places, Christ calls Him **by** the same name. **It is** known to many of you, that while the word which our Saviour used is very fitly translated by the English word Comforter, and while it unquestionably means *that*, it has been maintained **that it** means yet more ; and that some hint, some **suggestion**, of all the varied work of the Holy Spirit, is conveyed by that well-remembered word PARACLETE, which was actually used by Christ. We are too ready, all of us, to feel towards the mysterious Holy Ghost, something of the shrinking and the chill with which we naturally regard a disembodied spirit ; and superstition, and stupidity, and wicked mismanagement in childhood, have turned one of the words which make the name of that Blessed One, into a name of fear. But, brethren, if we did but get rid of our ignorant fancies; if we did but see the truth of the case; we should feel that there is something so kindly, something so homely and sympathising and dear, about that precious Holy Spirit, that surely, if He did but set right our sinful hearts, we never could think of Him but with perfect love and confidence: with that perfect love which casteth out unworthy fear. And what kindliness, what consideration, are in the very name by which the Saviour calls Him: "The Comforter, which is the Holy Ghost!" What a view of an unutterable love and patience is in that name, when you think it is a name of God! "The Comforter!" One who will not be impatient at our little griefs, and at the poor way in which we bear them: One who will condescend from the great movements and concerns of the universe, to think of all the little cares and sorrows of a poor human being,—of a feeble woman, or a little child, or a poor struggling anxious man with his weight of care and toil,—things that many another man would not take the trouble of listening to: One who will sit down by us in our sorrow, and whisper consoling thoughts into our ear,— yea, carry His blessed peace into our very heart,— that peace which the world cannot give,—that peace of God which passeth all understanding! Think, brethren, of a Being who, in all the glory of Godhead, yet chooses for His special resort the darkest dwellings and the saddest hearts, all that He may convey His own strong consolation and gracious cheer: not despising our little troubles,—and how little, we might blindly think, must they seem to Him: entering into them all with unfeigned sympathy: bearing with our fretfulness and our murmurings; not scolding us for grieving, or hardly telling us it is no matter: not ordering us to cease to mourn, but comforting us as one whom His mother comforteth: leading the wandering, rebellious soul gently back: and sanctifying through all!

And *that*, my friends, *that* is the fashion in which we ought to think about the Holy Ghost,—the Blessed Spirit of God. No doubt, He does many things besides comforting. He regenerates us, and makes us new creatures in Christ: He convinces us of sin, and enables us to believe in the Saviour: He sanctifies us day by day, making us in the end meet for glory: He begins, in short, our better life, and carries it on to its perfection: He teaches us to pray, and breathes true devotion into our hearts: yet it is meet and right that with all this, we should worship and seek Him by His gracious name of Comforter. It is not an unworthy thing, to call Him by that name, whereby Christ called Him; nor to think of Him, for a little, in that character. Now, brethren, think of a human being, who should devote himself to going about from house of sorrow to house of sorrow, all to comfort: who never would hear of **a mourning heart,** among rich or poor, but he set himself to console it, and that without the faintest suspicion of intrusiveness or fussiness: who had such a charm about him, **through his tender heart** and his kind face and his gentle persuasive **voice,** that he would in time win his way **to the con**fidence of the most hard and repellent **and self-con**tained, and make them feel he was their friend, **and** get them to talk **out** to him all their burdened **heart:** whom no fretfulness nor sullenness **could weary:** whom no sorrow nor grief could long **withstand with**out being lightened and hallowed: oh, what **a heavenly** mission would **that man's be! You would not be** afraid of a man like that! And surely, **if you feel** aright, you will feel nothing but love **and confidence** towards One **who is all** *that* and a **thousand times** more; and whose name and nature and **work are set** before us in words that should come **home so warmly** to sorrowful human **hearts, as the blessed, kindly,** sympathising Holy Ghost, **the great and good Com**forter!

And now, my friends, **I wish that we may rest for** a little while in the contemplation **of this great truth,** that the Holy Spirit **is the Comforter: that we may** see how far this truth will enable **us to understand and** to love as we ought, this Third Person **in the God**head. May He Himself, Spirit of all light **and truth,** order that all that **is** said may **be said truly and** worthily!

And first, when we speak of the Holy Spirit as the Comforter of Christ's people, see what this implies as to His knowledge of us, and of all our circumstances. My friends, before any one can comfort you, he must not only know you, but must know you well. He must know what sorrow or trouble it is that is pressing upon you : he must know so much about your nature and your affairs as to be able to understand how it is that *that* sorrow weighs on you so heavily; and what is the particular kind of feeling it awakes in you ; and what the thoughts and remembrances are that come most bitterly across you as you look round or look back. You know that the very kindest heart and the very best intentions, will not enable any one to offer you real comfort unless he knows and understands you well ; nay, that the lack of power to understand you, may cause the best intentioned human being so to speak and so to act towards you, as only to increase your grief instead of relieving it. Yes, it is a sad sight, to see an injudicious, meddling, well-meaning, ignorant person, trying to offer consolation to a mourning heart. And think, then, my friends, how intimately and thoroughly the great Comforter, who can comfort when no one else can, must know you and yours ! Let us speak humbly, brethren : but I cannot but say that not the name Creator, not the name Redeemer, seems to convey the idea of such thorough knowledge of us and of all about us, as the name of Comforter ! For the Comforter, to do His work aright, must know a great many very little things about us : must make Himself well acquainted with all those little things about them which mourners and sufferers are so ready to tell us about, and which are apt to be wearisome to even really kind people,—perhaps to almost all but those who have passed through the like experience themselves. He must know all those thoughts and feelings within you, in your days of sorrow, which you do not tell to another ; but yet which go so far to make up the sum of your real inward life. The very shade of feeling with which you hear of the blighting of your fondest hopes : or with which you bend over the dead face of one who is very dear to you : or with which you turn away from the home of your early love ;—all those things which you know words are so vain to convey to others ;—all those things He knows. You may be sure he understands you, and what you feel,—as strangers do not and cannot ;—as even those who are not strangers often most imperfectly do. There is no one, none, who is so at home under your roof : who is so thoroughly versed in all your circumstances, your anxieties, your feelings ; as the Blessed Spirit of God. When you look back, in seasons of sorrow, over your pilgrimage hitherto : when you turn over the faded letters in which past years are embalmed : when you read some record that wakens up those departed days, and that makes the old time come over you : then be sure of this, that little as most of those you know can understand your thoughts and feelings, the Holy Spirit the Comforter understands them all!

But there is more and better than this. The Blessed Spirit not only knows **us**, but Feels for us. *That* is implied in the fact that He stands to us in the relation of Comforter. You might imagine such a thing, as a Being of infinite knowledge looking on at all the movements of our minds, as we might look on at the movements of ingenious machinery, with curious interest and nothing more. You might imagine Him as looking, with the interest of the anatomist or the machinist, at the play of the fearful and wonderful enginery of thought and feeling within us, as we go on through the manifold cares and sorrows of this life: noting how in certain conjunctures of outward circum-stances certain phases appeared within: remarking how at one time the spiritual machinery played buoyantly and lightly, how at another it dragged wearily and slow, how again it seemed as though it would break down altogether, shattered and beaten: and only thinking, in the sight of all this, that it is all very strange. You might imagine Him as knowing all about us, yet not in the least feeling for us: if indeed there can be perfect or even imperfect knowledge without the insight which the electric sympathy gives. Or, you might imagine a great Spirit, infinitely exalted above us; seeing how little and insignificant are the things which vex and distress *us*, when compared with the great concerns of the Universe: and only wondering that we should make such an ado about so small a matter: wondering at our anxieties and our tears with a feeling midway between wonder and contempt. You know, my friends, *we* often do just *that*. When you see a little child in great distress, you remark, likely enough, that the cause of its distress is very small: is something that *you* would never think of shedding tears about: and unless you have a deeper insight into truth than most have, you are disposed rather to be impatient of all this sorrow: you are disposed rather to be angry that the little thing should be so foolish, than to feel any real, hearty sympathy with its distress. Ah brethren, if the Holy Spirit were like *us*, He would many a time rather chide than comfort!

But if it were so, He might retain many names of honour; but one name, kindly and heart-warming, would be His no more! If *that* were so, the Merciful Saviour would never have named Him, as "The Comforter, which is the Holy Ghost:" and though we might still adore Him from afar, we should not love Him as now; nor pray to have Him for the daily inmate of our homes and hearts! That He may comfort us, He must Feel for us: must look on at the sorrows of our hearts, not with the cold sharp glance of one that watches a strange machinery; but as with the kind, sympathetic look; and the beaming, glistening eye! That He may Comfort us, He must know that things, little in themselves, like to the great world or the great universe; are very great to us poor human beings: that a sorrow that never will be heard of five miles off, that never will be known of or cared for by a dozen fellow-creatures, may be a very great and crushing sorrow to a weak human heart. And what a view all this gives of His character : how near it draws Him to us : how well it makes us understand Him ! Think of the Third Person in the Godhead,—think of God the Holy Spirit,—all interested and concerned about a poor widow's anxious thoughts for her children,—all interested and concerned about a little child's tears : think of that Almighty One, feeling for a parent bidding farewell to a son who must go to a distant land,—feeling, heartily and truly, for the poor, faded mourner, weeping over the green grave ! O Gracious Spirit, teach us to know Thee, even as we are known !

And now we come to the third thing, the great thing, implied in the hopeful name which our Saviour, in the text, gives to the Holy Spirit. He understands us : He feels for us : and now, let us think, He comforts us. And see what *that* means. It means that He really succeeds in doing what human beings strive so vainly to do: in conveying comfort and consolation. He does not merely condole with us : He does not merely sit down by us and share our grief: He does not merely pity us : He Comforts us. And what skill, what delicate tact, what mighty power, what unspeakable tenderness, are conveyed and implied in that word ! You know the kind of way in which human beings sometimes think to comfort : and how cold and hard and worthless the consolation offered by such miserable comforters must seem to the sorrowful heart.   You may remember how Queen Elizabeth, with the best intentions I daresay, once wrote to a mother who had lost her son : and told her that she would be comforted in time ; and why should she not do for herself what the mere lapse of time would do for her ?   It would be felt as something like a mockery, I think : that hard, heartless saying.   It would, in a true heart, only make the present sorrow the sorer, to think that indeed it was to be outgrown : and, to the credit of our nature, let me say that I believe that with worthy people, great grief is never quite outgrown : it may leave us, but it does not leave us the men we were.   And you will think of Cicero's friend, writing a letter of condolence to the Roman philosopher after he had lost his daughter : and insisting, by way of comfort, that really the loss was a matter of no great consequence : asking, almost indignantly, how, when the Republic had fallen, Cicero could be so much afflicted for the loss of a single individual,—" a poor, little, tender woman :" these were the consoler's very words.   But it is not in these hard ways, that the True Comforter does His work !   It is not by upbraiding our nature's weakness : it is not by any process of logic : that that Heavenly Messenger accomplishes His blessed end.   It is rather by gentle soothing, we cannot say how : by presenting glorious and immortal hopes: by breathing resignation to the kind will of the kind Father above us: by sanctifying the affliction which has fallen, to wean our hearts from this troublesome world, and to set our affection above, where suffering, and sorrow, and change, and death, are done with for evermore! No doubt, my friends, the very fact that the name of Comforter is so dear, implies that Comfort is a thing we shall all often greatly need: no doubt, the law stands repealed as yet, that "through much tribulation we must enter into the kingdom of God:" but remember, brethren, that one great good of sorrow is this, that if we never knew it;—if we never knew what it is to have our hopes blighted and our hearts wrung;—we never should know, and never should love, as we ought, that Blessed One, who begins, carries on, and ends our Christian life!

And so, my Christian friends, I have sought, humbly yet most earnestly, to set before you one blessed character, one blessed work, of the Holy Spirit of God. I do not want you to think of a vague, mysterious Spirit, whom you can little comprehend: I want you to think of the kindly, homely Comforter, that sits down by a bereaved mother's side and carries consolation to her heart; and that dries the mourner's tears! I want you to remember, that in every kind heart, and every soothing voice, that is in man or woman over the face of this world; you have faint and far specimens of the Holy Ghost's kindest heart, and of His gentlest voice that speaks to the believer's soul! We can love and trust Him, Blessed Sanctifier and Comforter of all God's people; as we never could the mysterious Spirit, seen in absolute glory, and in no relation to ourselves. You have seen how much is implied in the name of Comforter, of kindly sympathy; of perfect understanding of us; of feeling for us in all we feel. Yea, after *that* Name like which there is none other: after the Name of SAVIOUR itself; there is no more precious one that human lips can ever speak: there is none at which human knee may more fitly bow! My dear friends, let us, every one of us, join this day in the hearty petition: Oh, Comforter of Christ's people: oh, Blessed Spirit who art God: come and comfort us on the way to rest: and sanctify us till we are meet for entering there!

> Dependent on Thy bounteous Breath,
>   We seek Thy grace alone;—
> Through childhood, manhood, age, and death,
>   To keep us still Thine own!

Nov. 30, 1862.

IV.

MAN COME TO HIMSELF.

"And when he came to himself"—St Luke xv. 17.

SOMETIMES, simple and familiar forms of speech express a great principle,—a great truth: and one, not distinctly understood by the people who use them. We have the very best reason to believe that the prophets who in old times were inspired by God to convey His message to mankind, did not always fully understand the meaning of the words they employed. And day by day, we, my friends, are all of us accustomed to speak in words whose direct and immediate force we understand ; but which imply a vast deal more than is always present to our mind when we speak them. We have an instance of this in the text to which I am to turn your thoughts at this time. It is a familiar form of speech, and a very short one : and, unlike some of the idiomatic phrases which you will find in our English translation of the New Testament, it stands the same in the Greek and in the English. So it is an idea that suggested itself to men's minds long ago : and it is a form of words that was in common use, as among us, so ages before we were born : this idea and this description of a man coming to his sounder reason, as of one who has " come to himself." And in that familiar phrase, there is a great and solemn truth implied and suggested to us : the great truth, that man is a fallen creature : that man needs to be set right : and that in order to be set right, what man needs is restoration to a pure and excellent ideal, which, for the present, is lost and gone.

You will be told by the Etymologist, who investigates the original meaning of words, that the first and most natural reference of the phrase which forms our text, is to the case of one who is recovered from a fainting-fit : when such a one is restored to consciousness and sense again, you say, He has come to himself. Then the phrase came to be used of one who, from a condition of mental unsoundness, was brought back to reason : of one, in whom the wayward, fitful, miserable estate of madness, was by God's blessing made to give place to a sound mind : you would say of him, He has come to himself. And then, by a farther extension of its signification, the phrase came to be applied to deliverance from any error or delusion ;—from any condition of mind which is wrong and morbid : so that you might say of one who has come out of some violent and degrading fit of passion ; or who has been emancipated from some foolish prejudice or absurd opinion ; that he has come to himself. But I ask you to observe, my friends, that in every case in which we use the phrase, it always means that the man has come

from a worse state to a better one. You never say of
a man doing or thinking foolishly or wrong, that he
has come to himself. But if a man be doing what is
right, and wise, and good, after having done what was
hasty and foolish and wrong;—then you say of *him*
that he has come to himself:—his better self indeed,
but his truer self too. And oh, brethren, how much
is conveyed to us by this deep natural belief, that un-
derlies this common phrase: the deep natural conviction, that so long as man is wrong, so long as man is
astray,—man is not himself!

And let us remember, this phrase, bearing this
meaning, and implying so much, is now stamped with
authority. We are entitled to take it, and build upon
it all it will bear. It has the mark upon it, that en-
titles it to pass current everywhere, as a genuine and
right way of thinking and speaking. Here, in the
text, we have words which proceeded out of the lips of
God. Our divine Saviour said them: May God's
good Spirit teach us rightly to understand them!
They come in, these comfortable and hopeful words,
in that blessed parable of the poor prodigal, for which
many a sinful wanderer has thanked God upon
bended knees: and which makes us understand, in
sober earnest, that the Almighty Judge above us, far
from desiring our punishment and destruction, is as
ready to welcome us, when we turn from our sins and
go back to Him, as the kind father who saw his poor,
starved, weary wanderer while yet a great way off, and

ran to meet him, and welcomed him to his heart again without one syllable of reproach.   Now, mark what is taught us by the text, coming where it does.   The poor prodigal was not himself throughout the earlier part of the story.   He was not himself when he came to his father, and asked the portion which he was so little fit to have or to use : and he was still less himself when he turned his back upon his home, followed by his father's anxious forebodings : and even less than that, when away in the far country, among his graceless companions, recklessly wasting the portion which his father had worked hard to win.   But, starving in the mighty famine : sitting, hungry, among the swine : a poor, ragged wretch, whose fair-weather friends had cast him off; to whom no man gave, and for whom no .nan cared : seeing now his sin and misery and want, and resolved to arise and return in penitence to his father, content if only received as a hired servant in the home where he had been a favoured son : now, my friends, the Saviour tells us,—now, the prodigal has come to himself!

Yes: it was when he did the first wise and right thing that we are told he did at all : it was when for the first time in all we are told of him, he reasoned and acted like a wise man and not like a fool : it was *then* that the wise Saviour, who knows what we are, so well, said that He had " come to himself!" Surely there is something hopeful, as well as something of solemn warning, here.   We have fallen far from what God made us: we are sinful, anxious, miserable, worldly, helpless: **yet,** through Christ's atoning **work,** through the Blessed Spirit's operation, we may be,—and if God's will be carried out in us, we shall be, **made** perfectly holy, and happy, **and** safe again: and when *that* good work is done **in us, it** will **not be** that we are **made** into anything more or better than **God at the first** designed us for: it will only be that we have attained the true **Ideal** of human nature,— **and been** glorified into **that** for which God when He **made** us intended us: **it will only** be, my friends, that **in** the noblest and truest sense of the phrase, we shall **have** at last " come to ourself!"

We take the text, then, as something to remind us, **that we have** fallen far, but not fallen hopelessly: that **great as is our** present depression beneath **the condition in which our race was created, so great** may yet **be our rise:** and **that** the very end and purpose of all **Christ's work** and suffering in this world, was to bring **us back to** our better selves **;** to restore **us to the holiness,** happiness, and peace, **which man lost when man fell.** And **if** this be so, my friends, **the subject to** which **I ask** your thoughts is not one wholly **sad.** If **a man has** met great worldly reverses **of** fortune : if, **from** having his children in comfort and affluence, he is obliged **now to** see them poorly fed, and barely clad : though he may oftentimes look back **upon** his better days, it will always be something **of a trial to do so:**

if there be no hope at all that these better days are to come back.   And still more, if a man have fallen into sin and shame, and if he be always sinking deeper in it, oh with what agony he will remember the time when he was innocent and esteemed: it will be unutterable bitterness to look up to the elevation he once held, now lost for ever: he will know how true is the poet's declaration, that "a sorrow's crown of sorrow is remembering happier things!"   And if it were so, spiritually, with you and me: if the state of sin and misery in which we are by nature, were a state from which we never could be delivered: if the pristine holiness and happiness we have lost, were lost for ever: if low as we are, we must always remain, and only go deeper and deeper down: then, my friends, the less we thought of the glory that is gone, the more content, with a dreary desponding contentment, we should be.   But for this end Christ lived and died; for this end the Holy Spirit labours day by day: that we may be delivered from the ruin, the sin and misery in which we are all sunk by nature; and brought back again to that holy and happy estate in which we thankfully though humbly recognise our true self. And in all we can discern of the holiness and happiness in which we were made, we discern the holiness and happiness to which, by God's grace, if we do but heartily consent to it and strive for it, we shall be raised up again! It was a beautiful morning that dawned upon our race, though it turned soon into a cloudy and

stormy day : and the cloudy and stormy day is drag-
ging slowly over us : but in the distant horizon there
is a light breaking, which shall yet grow into a day
more glorious and bright than ever shone upon us before : a day whose light shall never be overcast, and
whose sun shall never go down !

Let us remember, then, that the human race *was itself*, when it was at its best. Man *was himself*, before
he fell. And let us look back, to whence we are
fallen : that we may see to what we may yet rise again.
Let us try, this day, to make out the lineaments of our
true and better self : and to compare these with what
we are now.

I shall follow, in speaking of all this, the order suggested in a certain treatise, very familiar to most of
us from our childhood. We were created in God's
image : and our fall brought us into an estate of sin
and misery. Sin, and Misery : in these two things lies
our lost condition as we now are by nature : and let
us compare our present state, and our better state, in
these two respects.

As for sin, you know there is a double burden
there. Two things go to make the burden of our
sinfulness. There is, first, what is commonly called
Original Sin : not that I wish to make much use of
these phrases of technical Theology : I desire to
preach, not the metaphysics of the Gospel, but the
blessed Gospel itself : yet probably no phrase would
more compendiously set out the doctrine as to that

earliest burden of sinfulness we bear. So, by original sin, we are to understand the sinful nature we inherit: a nature which very early begins to shew its bent to evil rather than good: and likewise, the guilt of our first parents' primal sin, which in a very real sense is imputed to us,—that is, placed to our account, so that we have to answer for it, and suffer for it: as it is a matter of unquestionable fact we do. And the second thing which goes to make the burden of our sinfulness, is a thing which weighs much more heavily upon our conscience: it is, the countless actual sins we have done. Now, brethren, mark the difference between man as he is now, and man as he was when he was himself, as regards this double burden of sinfulness. Our first parents had no inherited burden of guilt. They started fair. We do not. They had not to bear that load which all of us have to bear: that load which crushes down many of our race,—and which many a one has hardly a hope of escaping. They had not, woven into their very constitution of body and mind, something that was to be always a clog, and oftentimes a sore temptation. And then, in that happy time, when man was right; he knew no actual transgression. He knew nothing of those manifold sins which press on your consciences; and press the more heavily the more your consciences are enlightened: all the manifold evil you have yourselves thought and done: all the good that you have failed to do. Now, what we need as regards all this, is to be brought back to our better self : brought back to where human nature was before it fell : and Christ, in His great atoning work, does *that*. He puts us, in the respect of the sinfulness into which we are fallen, in the condition in which our first parents were before they broke God's law. There is indeed one glorious difference. He puts His redeemed ones so effectually in that condition, that they can never leave it again. Not the unstable and speedily-lost purity of the days in Eden : but an enduring, an irrefragable holiness, never to be lost more !

You all know well, doubtless, the double operation whereby Christ takes away the double burden of sinfulness from His ransomed people. As for the burden of our actual sins,—as for their responsibility and their punishment ;—as for whatever responsibility may attach to us through the original load of guilt transmitted to us from Adam ;—as for all *that*, He takes it away, by bearing the punishment due for our sins,— by offering Himself, truly and actually, as a propitiatory sacrifice : a sacrifice so wonderful, so precious, so accepted by God, that it can blot sin out ; separate between the soul and its responsibilities : open a way in which the just and holy God can receive as innocent, can adopt into His family, the sinner,—cleared utterly from all the burden of his sins. Repent of sin,—and God's Spirit waits to help you to repent : Believe in Christ,—and God's Spirit waits to help you to believe : and no writing stands against you in God's book any more : God is content to look upon you, and see you clear and blameless, as Adam before he fell. " Being *justified* by faith, we have peace with God, through our Lord Jesus Christ." " There is therefore now *no condemnation* to them which are in Christ Jesus." " They are *without fault* before the Throne."

And as for the burden of our sinful nature,—of the heart within us averse to good and prone to evil,—*that* burden, too, through Christ's great atonement, is taken away by the working of the Holy Spirit. Through His regenerating power, the Christian is made a new creature in Christ Jesus : the perverse nature is replaced by a better and purer : a new heart is created within him, and a right spirit is renewed : and then, day by day, in the constant work of sanctification, the remaining evil is farther sapped, and subdued ; and the blessed fruits of the Spirit are made to appear,—the love, joy, peace, and all blessed graces, which never grew in the heart indigenously. It is a longer work, this, you know, than the single act of our justification : it is a work, the best believer knows, never fully carried out in this life : much remaining corruption lingers : and it is the most advanced Christian who feels this most deeply : but still, the work is doing ; and on the whole always progressing ; which will leave us at last with the soul unvexed by evil and temptation, as Adam's when he knew no sin.

And thus, my friends, as for the sin which makes the first great burden in our fallen state ; you see that even now, and here, the work is done, in part, which shall bring us back to the sinless state which is man's right state : the state in which man was made at the first, and to which every redeemed soul will be restored again. Even here, and now, in part : but when it shall not be here, but hereafter : not now, dimly and darkly, but then, face to face : when this weary, sinful world is left behind, and this troublesome, anxious life done with : and when not merely the guilt of sin is no longer resting upon us, but the power of sin is wholly dead : when the white, clear page shall bear nothing against us, and when our entire nature shall be pure, as God is pure : when evil shall have nothing more in us, or around us, or over us, or against us, than it had when man was fresh and glorious from his Creator's hand : surely then, indeed, in the fullest force of that most significant expression, man shall have been brought back to himself !

But there is more. The Fall brought us, not only into an estate of Sin, but into an estate also of Misery. And we remember from childhood the sad but too true tale of the items that make up human misery. We have lost communion with God. We lie under His wrath and curse. We are liable to the manifold ills and troubles of this life : to death, which ends our sojourn here in a fashion so painful and lowly : and then, to final woe. To all these things we are liable by nature : and you will think that misery is not too strong a word to express the condition of a keenly sentient and an immortal being, pressed by these.

Looking back, we discern a day when it was different: different in each one of these respects which we have summed up. Once, man walked in communion with God: and was free and happy in that communion. And you know, brethren, it is a certain fact, that that communion, and the love of that communion, are gone, now. Man, by nature, shrinks from God: shrinks from Him with vague mistrust and fear: the old way is lost! And when we are awakened to see things rightly, we feel that we deserve God's wrath and curse; that they are the necessary consequence of our sins; that we have nothing to say why they should not come down upon us: and how different *that* must once have been! In all Adam's consciousness there was not a thought or idea corresponding to these things. In his unfallen state, he would not have known what any one meant who had spoken to him of the wrath and curse of God: and least of all would he have been able to understand, till sad experience taught him, what is meant by the pangs of an accusing conscience;—what is meant by the burden of remorse; and by the deep overwhelming sense within, that God's wrath and vengeance are justly due. We need not dwell upon the sad assemblage which makes up the ills that flesh is heir to in this life: the anxieties, the cares, the disappointments, the bereavements, sickness, pain, weariness, and the load of forebodings and fears; ending only with death : and then, beyond death, something worse **than all.** But just think how different it once **was with** man in all these respects! No cares nor fears : no sickness, no want, no pain : no death: **and not** the faintest suggestion **of** following woe !

And now let us thankfully mark how the Redeemer takes away; **even here, in part,** and fully hereafter; **each of** these things that go to make **the** sum of the sorrow into which man **came** when he fell. **The lost communion** with God, He brings back. Once far away from God, and enemies to Him through wicked works, we are brought **near again** by the great Mediator ;—the Daysman, who can lay a hand upon both. Christ teaches us to love and trust God : because He makes us know God ;—shews us the Almighty, not in the obscurity and chill of His awful natural attributes,—not as the angry Judge whose laws we have broken,—but as the reconciled Father, holding out to us the arms of His love, and bidding the sinful wanderer return. Christ "hath declared" God: shewn us God : shewn us God in His own blessed character, and life, and death : and the more we know of God, the better shall we love God, and the more **confidingly trust Him.** And as for God's wrath and curse under which we lie by nature, *these* the Saviour hath taken away. **He has** Himself borne **the** punishment of our sins : the fiery wrath has exhausted itself upon our Substitute : and if we do but accept Him for our Substitute, it concerns us no more. The manifold ills and trials of life may still remain : but even in this world He lightens them, takes the worst sting from them : do but trust Him as we ought, and God will "keep him in perfect peace whose mind is stayed upon" Himself : and even where these ills and cares are most heavily felt, the Holy Spirit makes them work together for the soul's true good : uses them as discipline to make the soul meet for a better and holier world ; where they shall be felt, because they shall be needed, no more. As for the death which has "passed upon all men," because "all have sinned ;" we know that "our Saviour Jesus Christ has abolished death :" has changed its essential nature : has turned it to the messenger of peace ; has made it the dark portal which we bow the head as we pass under, and lift it upon the farther side, in the presence and the light of God ! And *there*, in that Beatific Presence, man will be happy as before he fell, and safer by far : he will be happy with a bliss which shall be absolutely complete ; and which never can be shaken, or lessened, or imperilled more !

And then, indeed, my friends, in that Golden City for which we look, all will be well again ! You know, Christians, that the work of restoring us to the early happiness, so soon lost, is far from being completed here. In a measure, Christ restores us to communion with God : in a measure, leads us to love and trust

God: yet cares remain, and death awaits; and fears may sometimes steal in of what lies beyond, in that undiscovered country from which no message comes back. For we are sinful, yet: and so long as we are sinful, we never can be perfectly happy. If Christ's faith and love be in us: if the Holy Spirit be working upon us: then we are in some degree restored to what we would be: but we are not yet brought to ourselves: not yet brought up to that pure and happy standard of being, which man can recognise as his true and unfallen self! But in that Better Land, where sin is done with, and sorrow is done with: where, through Christ's blessed work, the Fall is blotted out in both its dreary parts: where man is lifted up from the "estate of sin and misery" into which he fell: where we shall be holy as before, and happy as before, and safe as never before: then, brethren, there will be a glorious fulfilment of these words Christ spake of the Prodigal: then, truly and completely, man shall have "come to himself!"

Yes, my friends: in our Redeemer's presence,— if God, for His sake, bring us there: we shall be right; and right for the first time in all our pilgrim- age. It has been, since we were born, a long and sad series of errors, sins, and follies. The only approach to a sound mind that the wisest among us has ever shewn, has been in going to Jesus and believing on Him; if God has enabled us to do *that*. And think what blessed light this casts on our solemn parting from this world.   You remember how the ancient Greek poet spake of one of his heroes, lying dead: "There he lay, great and broad, having forgotten all his doings in this life."   Is it thus, my friends, we should speak of the departed believer? There lies his body, dead and cold.   Is his soul away from itself, in a swoon of dim forgetfulness? Nay, it is in the loving presence of God: it is clear and right at last: it has a sense of home it never felt before: kind voices welcome the believer, entering where he is now: dear friends gather round him. Think you, he is all astray, because he has gone forth from that familiar body and these accustomed scenes? Nay, brethren: in a truth never known in all his life before, the believer has "**come to himself!**"

V.

THE WELL-GROUNDED HOPE.

"And experience worketh hope."—Rom. v. 4.

So says the great apostle Paul: "Experience," he tells us, "worketh hope." Brethren, what does your own life's history say to that? You know, of course, that when any general principle like this is laid down;—when it is asserted that a certain discipline produces upon the soul of man a certain effect;—the way in which it must be decided whether the principle be true or not, is just to ask a great many human beings whether they have themselves found it so. It is a question of fact: and it must be decided by the testimony of competent witnesses. What we have to do is, not to argue that this or that training seems likely to work this or that result upon man's soul and heart. The question is, not whether experience ought to work hope: many things in this world ought to do, and are intended to do, what they fail of doing. The question is, Does experience work hope? And I am sure, my friends, that you will agree with me, that at the first glance. the apostle's assertion seems a startling one.

"Experience worketh hope." Ah, brethren, take that principle in its largest sense : apply it to the interests of this life and this world : and who is there that does not know that the apostle's statement would be utterly wrong? You have *not* found, we know, that the most experienced people are the most hopeful. You *have* found, that in this world, it is the inexperienced who are the most sanguine. Look at inexperienced youth, with its bright and glowing hopes. Compare it with age,—compare it even with manhood, with its sobered anticipations and views, the result of experience : and say whether experience has not wrought disappointment rather than success, and despondency rather than hope! The inexperienced man is all buoyant anticipation : he sees no difficulties in the way ;—he looks for brilliant success in life ;—he looks forward to a lot of perfect and unmingled happiness. How different with the man who has had some experience of the realities of life : how sober, and how modest, are his hopes of earthly happiness and success! Ah, how *he* has tamed down from the feverish fancies and high hopes of youth : how experience, in his case, has wrought anything rather than hope! *Once*, life was to be all romance, and fame, and happiness. *Now*, he knows that life must be sober prose, and humble work, and ceaseless worry. Who is there that does not sometimes, on a quiet evening, sit down and look back upon his early days, and his early friends ; and think sadly of the failures, the disappointments, the broken hearts, which have been among those who all started fair and promised well? And who is there, but must have sometimes found it difficult to believe that he himself, sobered, saddened, taken down by the wear of life and its many disappointments from the vain fancies and idle anticipations of that time, is indeed the self-same being! It cannot be doubted that there is one sense in which all after-life may be said to be a disappointment. It is far different from that which it was pictured by early anticipations and hopes. The very greatest material success still leaves the case thus. Though you reach the very place, the very lot, on which your heart was set, you are sure to find it something quite different from what you fancied when you set your heart upon it. Yes, brethren, when you look to this life and this world, you might well think that St Paul was mistaken when he wrote the words of the text. You might well think that he was attributing to experience an effect the very opposite of that which it in fact produces. You would say that "experience worketh" sobriety of expectation : that "experience worketh" disappointment : that "experience worketh" despondency : yea, that sometimes "experience worketh" despair itself : but surely never, never, that "experience worketh *hope!*"

Yes; and you would say right. Earthly experience sobers earthly hope. But it was not of earthly experience that the apostle spake; nor of earthly experience that the apostle spake; nor of

earthly hope. There is no doubt at all, that the more
you know of this world, the less you will hope from it.
The more experience you have of the things of sense
and time, the less expectation you will have that *they*
will ever make you happy. But there are interests,
there is a world, there is a Being, concerning whom
the more you know, the more you will hope and expect. As regards our Blessed Saviour, His grace, and
preciousness, and love: as regards the solid peace
and happiness to be found when we find a part in
His great salvation: as regards the sanctifying and
comforting influences of the Holy Spirit: as regards
the power and prevalence of earnest prayer: as
regards the rest and refreshment the weary soul may
find in a Lord's-day duly sanctified: as regards
the consolation which religion can impart amid
earthly disappointments, sorrows, and bereavements:
as regards the peace that Christ can give in death:
as regards His power to take the victory from the
grave, and to turn the heathen *burying-place* into
the Christian *sleeping-place:* as regards such things
as these, " experience worketh hope :" the more
you know of Jesus, His promises and His grace,
the more you will expect from Him ; and instead of
experience leading us to say, as it does lead us
to say of most earthly things, " I have tried it; I
have fairly tested it ; it cannot make me happy ; I
shall trust it no more :" experience of God leads us
rather to say, " I know Whom I have believed, and

am persuaded that He is able to keep that which I have committed to Him against *that* day :" " I love the Lord, because He *hath* heard my voice and my supplication : because He *hath* inclined His ear unto me, therefore will I call upon Him as long as I live :" " The Lord *hath been* mindful of us : He *will* bless us still !" Yes, the apostle was right. In the sense in which he used the words ; and in the matter of those great spiritual interests of which he was thinking when he used the words : true it is and unquestionable, that " experience worketh hope !"

And so, my friends, it comes to be, that the reception which such a general principle as that stated in the text will get from any human being, depends mainly upon what kind of being he is : upon what kind of thoughts are uppermost in his mind : upon what class of interests hold the first place in his heart. Thus, if you go to a man whose whole heart and mind are set upon this world ; whose first thoughts run upon how he is to get on in life,—upon temporal success and earthly ambition and happiness : if you go to him, and tell him that " experience worketh hope ;"—assuredly he would say to you, No : anything but that ! For he will involuntarily and at once test the principle by considering whether it holds true in regard to those things about which *he* thinks most, and most earnestly : and he will feel at once that it does *not* hold true there : that indeed as regards worldly hopes and fancies you could hardly say anything more thoroughly false than

that experience confirms, and satisfies, and encourages
them: that in very truth, as regards worldly things,
"experience worketh" the very reverse of "hope."
But go to the man who has laid up his treasure above,
and set his affection *there:* go to the man in whose
heart the Saviour holds the first place: go to him who
feels that this world is the dream and the shadow, and
that the waking, earnest, solemn realities that concern
immortal beings such as we are, lie beyond the grave:
go to such a one, and tell *him* that "experience worketh
hope." And you may rely upon it, *he* will agree with
you at once: for he will test your principle by considering whether it holds true in regard to those things
which *he* regards as the most solemnly important: and
he will remember that his Saviour's sufficiency, and
grace, and love, often tried, have never failed: that
he never yet has found that the Lamb of God is not
able to take away all sin: that he never yet has found
the day in which the Blessed Spirit is not able to comfort and sanctify: that he never yet has been made to
feel that Christian peace, and charity, and joy, are all
a fond delusion: but rather he has found, in his own
experience, that the longer he has gone on in the service of his God and Saviour, the more entirely satisfied
he is with it: that the longer he has loved and trusted
the Blessed Redeemer, the more reason he sees for
loving and trusting Him: that the longer he has prayed,
the more heartily and hopefully he can go to the throne
of grace in Christ Jesus' name: that the more he has

known of God, and God's service, and God's dealings with His children, the more thoroughly and confidingly can he leave himself and all he holds dear in his God's kind and almighty hand : that he has "tasted and seen that God is good :" that he needs no man's testimony to assure *him* what kind of Master he serves, what kind of Saviour he rests upon : that he has tried for himself : that he has learned by experience : and that true it is in the letter and the spirit, that "experience worketh hope !"

So you see, that the same life, the same events, the same experience, may work upon the soul effects directly opposed to each other ; according as the soul's own nature may be. If this world have the upper hand in the soul, then experience will work disappointment and despondency. If the unseen world have the upper hand in the soul, then experience will work hope. And it is not a thing out of the analogy of nature, that the same agent should work contrary effects, according to the nature of the thing it acts on. You will think of the often-recurring comparison of the Middle Ages : Fire, the same fire, hardens clay and softens wax : and even so experience, the same experience, works hope in the spiritual man, and disappointment in the worldly man.

And now, brethren, in thinking for a little space longer concerning St Paul's declaration, that "experience worketh hope ;" let me suggest to you two thoughts, which are implied in the apostle's principle, and which are the great reasons why the apostle's principle is true.

These are, that in the great concern of religion, you are sure, if you seek in the right way, to get what you seek : and you are also sure, when you get what you seek, to find it equal your expectations.

It is because Christian experience proves these two facts, that Christian experience worketh hope. And it is because worldly experience proves the reverse of these two facts, that worldly experience works disappointment and an unwillingness to cherish hope.

First, then, in the great concern of religion, you are sure, if you seek in the right way, to get what you seek.

Now here, at once, we find a point in regard to which there is a total contrariety between worldly things and spiritual things. Who is there that needs to be told, that one great cause of human disappointment in worldly things lies in this: that however anxious you may be to get some thing on which you have set your heart, and however diligent you may be in using all the means which you think tend towards your getting it, you may yet entirely fail of getting it? You may be eager to grow rich : you may feel most vividly the many comforts and advantages and refinements which wealth can buy : you may toil early and late to accumulate a fortune : and yet you may never do more than maintain your family in decent respectability ; or you may even know the bitterness of poverty and want. You may be eager to gain eminence and distinction : you may think how fine a thing it would be to make your kindred proud when your name is mentioned ; to be known by what you have done, or said, or written, to many human beings who otherwise never saw or knew you, and whom you will never see or know : and yet your ambition may be so sorely out of proportion to your abilities, or circumstances may so hold you down, that you may continue nameless and obscure. Indeed, I daresay you have remarked, that those people who have set their whole heart upon any particular thing, are generally the very last to get it : we have all known of poor disappointed men who all their life were eagerly seeking for some desired object, and seeking in vain ; while that desired object was pressed upon other men, who cared very little about it. Yes, in the concerns of this world, you never can be sure, however anxious you may be to get a thing, and however hard you may work to get it, that you *will* get it after all. And so, as you gradually find this out by bitter experience, experience will be found to work disappointment ; but never, never hope. But in the grand concern of religion, all that is changed. In the grand concern of religion, if you seek diligently, and seek in the right way, you are sure to get what you seek. For *here*, the promise holds without a restriction or exception, "Ask, and it shall be given you: seek, and ye shall find: knock, and it shall be opened to you." We know, of course, that every promise that prayer shall be answered, must be understood as with the condition, provided the thing prayed for be for your own real good and for God's glory. And as we never can be sure, in the case of any earthly blessing, that it is for our own real good and for God's glory that we should get it; so we never can be quite sure that we shall get it, even in answer to the most earnest and persevering prayer. Not health, but sickness, may be the true blessing: not wealth, but poverty: not success, but disappointment: not the happy domestic circle, but the cold and lonely fireside. But when we pray for spiritual blessings: for repentance towards God and faith in Christ and a sanctifying Spirit;—we may pray with the absolute certainty that our prayer will be granted, because we pray with the absolute certainty that we are asking *that* which it will be for our good to get, and for God's glory to give. And thus it is, that if we seek grace and mercy and peace, in humble prayer through Jesus: if we set our heart upon spiritual gifts and graces, and strive after them in the appointed way: if we set our heart upon obtaining that saving interest in the Blessed Lamb of God, which is the most precious of all possessions: if we set our heart on putting down the evil that is in us, and growing in holiness day by day: if we set our heart on reaching that confiding faith in

God which trusts Him with everything, and in that finds perfect peace : oh brethren, if we set our heart upon these things, sure as God liveth we shall find them : if we earnestly wish for them, and strive after them, we shall assuredly call them our own : we shall feel their solid reality ; we shall feel their peace in us day by day : and as our own experience assures us of all this, we shall feel how truly the Apostle spake, who said that as for God, and God's grace, and God's promises, and God's great salvation, "experience worketh hope !"

Yes, my friends : seek spiritual blessings ; and seeking, you shall find. You will never need, here, to resign your mind, as you may, to sore disappointment and failure. You will never need to sit down in sadness and say,—I longed for pardon, and I prayed for it and strove for it,—but God in His wisdom saw meet to refuse it me : I longed for holiness, I prayed and strove for it,—but God saw that it was not good for me, and He said I must do without it : I longed for Heaven, I have prayed and striven all my life for it,—but perhaps God sees that it will be best for me never to enter into that quiet Home. You have said the like, many times, over the wreck of your worldly hopes. You have sometimes had to say,—Well, I set my heart on *that:* and I toiled for it hard as man could toil · I did my very best : but God's will be done, I shall not get it,—I shall never get it. But in regard to the great essential blessings of the Gospel, experience will teach its lesson, experience will do its work : and it never will work disappointment : it will always work hope.

But we said that another fact on which the principle in the text founds, is, that in the matter of spiritual blessings, you are sure, when you get what you seek, to find it equal your expectations.

It is but the first and earliest view of the disappointment which comes of longer experience of this world, to regard it as a feeling arising from our so often failing to get the worldly thing on which we had set our hearts. There is a further and deeper disappointment than *that*. It is the disappointment of the man who reaches the place he longed for,—who gets the thing he desired,—and then finds that it will not make him happy : that to possess it takes off the enchantment which was lent by distance : that it is far, very far, from being what he had deemed it, possibly through long laborious years. Ah, my friends, is not *this* disappointment felt everywhere : does it not begin to be felt early ? When you were schoolboys, longing for the holidays, what vague, delightful visions of perfect happiness were wrapped up in the mention of their name ! But the holidays came, as all holidays have done and will do : and in a few days you were heartily wearied of them. How many pushing business-men fancy they will be perfectly happy when they retire from business and settle in the country: and what a comment upon such fancies is the fashion in which retired men of business often haunt the places of their former toils like unquiet ghosts! They have got the rest they wished and worked for: they have got the pleasant country home: but they find, with sad disappointment, that these things are not at all what they had fancied them. *That* is the way of this world. Only to possess a thing, takes away half its value: the coveted eminence, position, mode of life, may still appear desirable enough after they have been reached; but they are not what fancy had painted them: and as worldly experience tells us *that*, it works the reverse of hope. But, brethren, when we turn to spiritual blessings, how different is it there! Once gain *them*, and they will never disappoint you: *They* will never fall short of the bright anticipations which you had formed of all they would be! And so far from it being the case, that to gain them and possess them cuts down their value, it is rather true that only those who have actually tried and possessed them are able to understand their worth. Oh, you may talk of the peace of believing, to the man who has never believed: you may tell of the preciousness of the Redeemer, to the soul that has never turned to Him: you may speak of the strong consolation of the Blessed Spirit, to him who has never experienced all the comfort He can impart: but your words will wake no response in the heart: they will seem an idle tale : you will be speaking in language hardly understood, and not felt at all. But speak of such things to the soul that has gained them and tried them : speak to the Christian sufferer of comfort in affliction, vouchsafed from above : speak to the humble believer of the Saviour's kindly sympathy and mighty power : speak to the aged pilgrim of the kind guidance of his God,—of a rod and staff which shall sustain the failing steps even in the last dark valley that must be trodden : and you will see by the beaming face and the glistening eye that you are talking of things thoroughly understood, and appreciated by an experience of them that worketh never-failing hope. He had thought that peace and pardon and joy in Christ would be good and happy things when he first resolved to seek them : but *how* good and happy, how satisfying and sustaining, till he had tried them for himself he never knew !

Yes, my friends, there *are* possessions which, when you gain them, will never fall short of your expectations of them. There *is* a happy home, into which the soul that enters, will never look round with disappointment, mortified that this is all. There never was the human being who said, I was earnestly desirous to gain the favour and friendship of God : to gain the good part in Christ : I strove and prayed to gain them : and now I have gained them, I find they are no such great matter after all : the prize is hardly worth the cost. God is ndeed my father : Christ is indeed my Saviour: the Holy Spirit dwells within my breast; and I know that heaven is my home: but these things leave me still unsatisfied and unhappy. No, brethren; experience never brought any human being to such a mind as *that*. *That* is the strain in which experience has taught men to speak of earthly ends, after they were won. Many a man has said, I laboured to grow rich; I thought I should be happy then: I have grown rich; and I am no happier than before. Many a man has said, I laboured to grow eminent; I thought I should be happy then: I have gained what I wished; and I am no happier than before. But the man never breathed who would say the like of the blessings of grace. The man never breathed who would say that he had grown weary of his Saviour's love and of the Blessed Spirit's consolation: that he had tried them for himself, and found them empty and vain! Nay: but rather those happy souls who have experienced most of the pure joys of religion, can testify that there is a solid reality about them which no words can express: that they can compensate for the want of all earthly possessions; but that no worldly treasures could make up for the loss of *them*. Hear what a Christian man once said on one of the last days of his life: " When I formerly read Bunyan's description of the land Beulah, where the sun shines and the birds sing night and day, I used to doubt whether there was such a place: but now my own experience has convinced me of it, and it infinitely transcends all my previous conceptions." What say you to *that*, my friends, for a comment upon our assertion, that the blessings of redemption once attained, will not fall short of that which we expect!

And now, as our meditation draws to a close, we look once more at these words, very few indeed, but very rich in meaning, wherein the great apostle tells us human beings, sobered even if not saddened in our anticipations of what this life will yield us, that "experience worketh hope!" No doubt, even as regards this world, this is true to a certain degree. The experience of many days has taught us to hope that the sun will rise to-morrow: that these short days will lengthen to the golden summer: that the seasons will bring back the flowers, and the green leaves return. But experience has not taught us to hope that there shall be to us fulfilment of the vague, bright anticipations of childhood, of the gay hopes of youth. We know better than to expect very much of this world now: experience has abundantly taught us that God's Word is right, when it tells us that this is not our rest,—that the home and the happiness of the immortal spirit, are far away. You *may* reach worldly success, my friends: I heartily wish you all of it that God sees good: but however happy your home may be, however prosperous your lot, experience will work you bitter disappointment if you think to find your soul's abiding portion amid the things of sense and time. "Thou madest us for Thyself," I think of St Augustine's words: "Thou madest us for Thyself; and our souls are restless till they find rest in Thee!" But, blessed be God's name, experience can work hope, better by far than the hopes of youth: calm, lasting, sober, yet glorious hopes: hopes of possessions that will not elude our grasp, nor wither in it: hopes that will sustain in life, and gladden even in the valley of death's dark shade. The worldly man, doubtless, thought he was saying much for his sanguine, hopeful spirit, when he said, "While I breathe, I hope." But the believer can say more than *that:* he can say, "When I draw my parting breath, still I hope!" The experience which has shattered his hopes of worldly happiness, has taught him that he never can hope too much of his Saviour's faithfulness, and love, and power. And say, brethren, which is the most truly hopeful human being,—the one who hopes just because he has no experience, or the one in whom experience has worked hope! Oh that we may so know Him in whom we have believed, that we may be persuaded that He is able and willing to keep us against that day! Oh that we may have that experience of our God and Saviour, which shall work in us a living faith, and a never-failing hope!

VI.

NOTHING WITHOUT CHRIST.

"Without Me ye can do nothing."—St John xiv. 5.

THERE never was but one being who wore the appearance of human nature, who had the right to say such words. It would have been great presumption in any mere man to have said to his fellow-creatures what Christ here says to his apostles, "Without Me ye can do nothing." It has been said with great truth, that in this world no man is necessary: there is no man in the world whom the world could not do without. There are many men who if they were taken away would be missed: would be very much missed, perhaps, by more or fewer human beings. But there is no man but what we may say of him, that useful and valuable as he may be, we might sooner or later,—we might with more or less difficulty, come to do without him. It is a truth this which we do not like to admit, perhaps, even to ourselves: there is not one of us, it may be, but cherishes the belief that if we were taken away, there would be some hearts where we should always be remembered and always missed,—where our absence would be regarded as an irreparable loss: we like to fancy that things would not go on exactly the same without us as with us. But this world has never seen more than one Being who could think, and who could say with truth to those connected with Him, that it was absolutely impossible for any thing or any person to make up for the want of *Him*: that it was absolutely impossible to go on when separated from Him. We come at last to live on just as before, though we may be parted from our nearest and dearest earthly friends. The little child fancied, when its mother died, that all the world was now a dreary blank, and that without her it could " do nothing:" but as weeks and months passed on, it learned that it *could* live, somehow, though it saw a mother's face, and heard a mother's voice no more : and after years have rolled away, the grown-up, busy man, hardly seems ever to remember at all her whom the heart-broken child missed and mourned so sorely. And the mother, in like manner, may feel her heart almost broken when her little one is called to go : may fancy that now all interest is gone from life,—and that without that little one she " can do nothing:" but time brings its wonderful easing : and at length her daily duties get back their interest ; and, though not forgetting, she gets on much as before. And it is the same way in every earthly relation. The husband comes to do without his dead wife ; and the wife to do without the departed husband. The congregation that missed their minister for a while, come at length to gather Sunday after Sunday with little thought of the voice it once was pleasant for them to hear. The state comes to do without its lost political chief, and the country without its departed hero : and we learn in a hundred ways, that no human being is absolutely necessary to any other human being. We may indeed fancy so for a while : but at length we shall find that we were mistaken : we may indeed miss our absent friends sadly and long ; but we shall come at last to do without them.

And so it would have been presumption and ignorance for any mere human being to have said such words as those of our text. It would have shewn how vain an idea he had of his own importance :—how far astray he was in his estimate of his own usefulness and worth. Here we find our Blessed Saviour saying to His apostles on the eve of parting from them,—saying without limitation or restriction,—that they could not do without Him,—that they could do nothing without Him. He sets no exception to the broad assertion He makes : He tells them that they could no more do without Him, than the branches could bear fruit if cut off from the parent tree : that at no place in all their wanderings,—at no hour in all their lives,—could they ever come to miss Him less than in the first pang of parting. They would not even be able, when separate from Him, to do as we can do when first parted from those we love,—to go through the duties that cannot be avoided, in some kind of cheerless, heartless way.

No: they would be absolutely paralysed and power-less. "Without Me," he says ;—"Without Me ye can *do nothing!*"

Now that we may come to a clearer understanding of our Saviour's meaning when He spoke these words, let us think what it is that we mean, when we say that we can *do without* any person. We understand, generally, that we can get on quite as well with our duties and our enjoyments, when he is away, and when we are without his advice, his help, his company. We understand, that we shall be just as happy, though we never see him at all : and that we shall get on with all we have to do just as well, though he be not there to advise us or to aid us. And when Christ said to His disciples, "Without Me ye can do nothing," He meant that as regarded Him, it was just the reverse of all this, and even more than the reverse of all this. He meant that they could not be happy away from Him ;—that they could not do the work to which they were called, away from Him ;—even that they could not do a single right thing but by a wisdom and a strength which they derived from Him and through Him ;—that in short, in the largest sense of the phrase, they could not " do without Him." " Without Me ye can do nothing :" and these words imply something quite different from,—something very far beyond,— the mere help and advice which one human friend can give another. When Christ said such words to His disciples, He meant far more than just that when He was gone, they would miss Him so much, they would feel so sunk and sad without Him, that they would be ready to sit down and dream over the pleasant past, rather than set themselves earnestly to the toils of the work-day present.   He was not thinking just of the sentimental sadness, (right and fit though it be,) which unnerves us and unfits us for duty when first separated from all we love.   It would be quite an exaggerated description to say that even one parted from home and friends and native country,—from everything he cared for upon earth,—was as hopelessly and as permanently unfitted for duty as a branch cut off from the vine is for bearing fruit.   He might be so for a while at first, but he would get over it : while the branch parted from the vine bears fruit no more. And I am going to take it for granted, without stopping to prove it at length, that though the words of our text were first spoken to the apostles, with special reference to the great work which lay before them, and in which they could do nothing without Christ ; still these words hold true no less of all Christians, in all times, in all places, and in all duties.   "Without Me," says Christ to us all ;—"Without Me ye can do nothing."

And towards a further understanding of what our Redeemer meant when He said these words, let me remind you that these words are spoken to true Christians only : they describe the condition of true Christians only.   Without Christ, it is a fact of ex·perience as well as a doctrine of scripture, *they* can do nothing. By the very necessity of their being they can do nothing without reference to Christ. Everything they do, they ought to do with an eye that looks beyond the immediate work itself, to Him. There should be a reference to Him in all their common toils. For His laws, for His sake, they should, they can, they must, do the least as well as the greatest thing. And more especially as to spiritual things they can do nothing without Him. They can do nothing but by wisdom and strength and grace of His giving. Now we ask you to remember this restriction on the general meaning of the text, that it is spoken to true Christians only. We wish it were universally true: we wish that no man could do anything without Christ. Then indeed it would be well for our straying race; for being compelled at every turn to feel our need of Him, we might be constrained to seek earnestly that we might "win Christ and be found in Him." And it is indeed a sad thing that so many men can do so many things without Him. · Without Christ the worldly man can do everything he does. Without Christ he can make money: without Christ he can push his way onward in life, till the unknown clerk becomes the great and flourishing merchant: "without Christ he can do" many a thing: without Christ he can live; without Christ he can die. Yet true as all this is, there is a sense in which the text may be applied even to worldly men. *The* great work of life, as you all know, is to work out our salvation : The one thing needful is an interest in the Atonement of Christ. The grand thing we have got to do in this world is to prepare for the next : to get ready for death, and judgment, and eternity : and we can say with perfect truth that the man who passes out of life without having done *that,* has *done nothing,*—nothing worth the reckoning ;—or to use a common phrase which aptly enough illustrates our assertion, nothing to speak of. Now without Christ no man can do anything towards *that :* without Him you can do nothing towards your own salvation : and so without Him even the worldly man can do nothing that is worth talking of : nothing that is worth counting as the work of a being destined to an endless life : nothing that is in the least proportion to his immortal nature : nothing that is not too insignificant to speak of, when we look upon it as the sole doing of a being that has left life's great task undone ! Ah, brethren, though the worldly man may think he is working hard in this world, and without Christ doing many things ;—he will own upon his death-bed,—he will own yet more when he enters the next world,—that he has done *nothing ;*—nothing that will count as anything *there !* He will feel *then,*—you will every one of you feel *then,* if you never felt it before, —that in the highest and truest sense, without Christ any of us " can do nothing !" Oh brethren, think of the man that never believed in Christ, entering the next world ; and there called to give an account of his stewardship,—asked what has he done : do you think he would dare, when bidden to render "an account of himself to God," to answer,—I made so many thousand pounds ;—I left a name that people on earth are talking of: I lived a cheerful, comfortable life ! Or would he not feel that it would be insulting the Almighty, even to mention such things as these as the doings of his time on earth : would he not feel all these things vanishing like shadows in the light of eternity,—would he not feel that all these things go for nothing *there:* would he not feel that if he has not "worked out his salvation," and believed savingly in Christ ; then in very deed he has "done nothing !"

It must be evident at once, that since without Christ we can do *nothing,* it would be an endless task were I to set myself to pointing out to you the various things which without Christ you cannot do. A list of such things would be a list of all things which are worth reckoning as the doing of a rational and immortal being. Still it has seemed that the most profitable way in which we can direct our thoughts in dwelling on this subject, will be to look at one or two selected things, in the case of which we more especially feel that we cannot do them without Christ.

And it is hardly needful to remind you, as the first and most important of these, of the working out of our salvation,—the first and greatest work which every human being has to do. I need not tell you that

without Christ we can do nothing as regards *that.*
You know that St Paul indeed tells us to "work out
our own salvation with fear and trembling ;" and if you
stopped reading the verse at that point, you might
think that this was something which we could do for
ourselves, in our own strength and wisdom : but as if
to prevent our fancying anything so far wrong, the
apostle goes on to add, "For it is God that worketh
in you both to will and to do of His good pleasure."
To obtain the forgiveness of our sins,—to obtain the
purification of our. heart, the sanctification of our
nature,—is a thing towards which we can do nothing
without Christ. It is the work of God's grace if we
are even brought so far as to feel that something must
be done to make our peace with Him,—that we must
see to it in earnest how we are to escape from woe
and rise to heaven when we come to die : But when
once the soul is brought to this state of anxious
inquiry,—when it comes to put the momentous
question, "What must I do to be saved ;" it must
feel indeed that without Christ it can do nothing.
There is no pardon, no peace, no hope, away from
Him. Oh brethren, just for a moment think of it,—
what could we do, if we were convinced of sin by
God's Spirit,—if we were made to feel that we had
sinned against God times without number,—if we
read in our Bibles the fearful denouncements of God's
wrath against sinners,—and if we knew nothing of
Christ or of salvation through Him ! What could we
do without Him ? Where *could* we turn ? The first

thing that perhaps we should think of would be an external reformation,—would be to set ourselves to avoid sin for the future: but even if a week's or a day's trial did not suffice to convince us that we *can-not* avoid sin ;—even if we did not read in our Bibles that "whatsoever is not of faith, is sin," and so that every action is sinful which is done without Christ ;—even if we could begin in our own strength to-day, and never sin more till we die ;—how are we to blot out our past sins? What can we do by ourselves towards having *them* forgiven? It is trite and commonplace at this time of day to repeat, that you do not pardon the criminal his past offences, merely because he promises to offend no more. And it is sad indeed to think what shifts men have had recourse to, when they tried to get pardon for past sin without Christ. It is sad to think of the punishments they have heaped upon themselves on earth, to anticipate and escape God's wrath in another world: of the penances, the scourgings, the fastings, the cold and nakedness, of the bed of thorns, of the weary pilgrimages, which even men calling themselves Christians have resorted to, when they sought "without Christ to do" something towards their soul's salvation. O brethren, there never were people more in earnest to get the pardon of their sins, and to get a title to happiness when they died, than the poor benighted Hindoos who have climbed over the sharp flints on their bare knees,—who have severed themselves from all human nature loves, and

heaped upon themselves all it loathes and shrinks
from, that thus they might get mercy from God.   But
oh ! without Christ what is all this worth ?   Unless
that Bleeding Lamb of God takes away our sins, they
never can be taken away,—they must cling to us for
ever.   Unless Christ "tastes death" for us, we must
drink the bitter cup ourselves : unless He bears the
penalty of the broken law, we ourselves must bear it
in woe for ever !   Without Him ;—without His atonement, His grace, His Spirit, we can do nothing towards our own salvation ; and when our eyes are
opened to our sinfulness, we must just sit down in
despair !   Only His blood can wash away our sins :
only His righteousness can justify us : only His Spirit
can sanctify us: and the further the believer has
travelled on his heavenward path, the more deeply he
feels how truly the Redeemer spake the words,—
"Without Me ye can do nothing !"

I desire to appeal to the experience of Christ's
own people, when I mention a thing in which we
learn day by day that without Him we can do nothing.   This is joining in His worship, and partaking
of His ordinances.   I would more especially allude
to the Sacrament of the Lord's Supper.   You all
know that without any help from Christ beyond the
common aids of His providence, a man may come to
church on a Sunday, and sit down there, and join in
the psalm, and look devout at the prayer, and listen to

the sermon. And you know too that in like manner, we may by ourselves come to the communion-table and partake of the elements which represent the body and blood of the crucified Redeemer. But I am quite sure, my Christian friends, that you have learned by experience that in such things as these, without Christ you can do nothing. Mere understanding without feeling,—mere head without heart,—will not do in the worship and in the ordinances of God. And it is no skill of ours that can waken in our bosoms that unearthly fire, that glow of heartfelt devotion, which we have sometimes felt as we sang God's praises or poured out our hearts in prayer, and which made us know what it is that is meant by "worshipping God in spirit and in truth." I am quite certain that the experience of every true Christian must have taught him to feel when he begins to offer prayer, "Now here is something which by myself I cannot do: Here I am endeavouring to do something in which without Christ I can do nothing: It depends entirely on whether He is with me or not, whether I am to feel my heart warmed and my soul lifted up to God in confiding happiness ; or whether I am to feel depressed and gloomy, even as the sunshiny landscape grows chill and dark when the sun is hidden by a cloud." How cold and dreary and heartless the worship of God's house would be without Christ! What a lifeless form is the Holy Sacrament, unless Christ meet with us at His Table!

I doubt not, my Christian friends, that sometimes when you have been holding communion with Christ in prayer, even on the bed of pain, or through the long watches of the sleepless night, you have felt a peace and a happiness which you would not give away for all the wealth of the world. And sometimes,—would to God it were always,—you have felt the Blessed Spirit breathing on your soul as you bent the knee; and as you poured out all your heart with a child-like confidence in your heavenly Father's ear, you have felt that Christ in very deed was with you. Or in the house of prayer, under the simple preaching of the unsearchable riches of Christ, you have felt your soul drawn out towards Him in a way which is to be felt but not described. Or at the Redeemer's table you have held holy communion with Him,—you have been able to cast all your cares upon Him, to leave yourself unreservedly in His hands,—to realise the meaning and to take the peace of the blessed promise so often forgot, that "*all* things shall work together for good to those who love Him:" and then upon the mount of ordinances you have felt so peaceful and so happy, that you almost wished, like the apostles on the hill of the Transfiguration, that here you might build your tabernacle, and go down no more from that pleasant elevation above your every-day temptations, and sins, and sorrows. And I doubt not, too, my believing friends, that in your experience there have been seasons of desertion, when the Saviour's felt presence was withdrawn; when your prayers were offered with little heart or comfort; when you no longer felt the house of God like the gate of heaven; when in the world within the breast, it was all dreary and desolate. And yet, sad as these seasons are, let us thank God for them.. If it were not that they sometimes come, we should forget how simply dependent we are upon Christ for all the comfort and benefit of His ordinances and His service: and thus we would welcome the dreariest night, so only it made us feel, more deeply than ever we had felt before, that "without Christ we can do nothing!" Oh, surely in a higher sense than even that of the sublimest of poets, the believer may take up his words: "I feel the stirrings of a gift divine: Within my bosom glows unearthly fire, Lit by no skill of mine!"

We might go on to point out to you, my friends, several other passages in our life in which we can do nothing without Christ: we might point out to you how union with Him is the source of every good deed that deserves the name: how His presence is the thing that shall "save us from the hour of temptation;" that shall comfort us under all our trials, and strengthen us for all our duties, and promote our growing sanctification and meetness for His immediate presence above. We might point out to you how "without Christ we can do nothing" towards reclaiming the spiritual "waste places of the earth,"—how His name, His Cross, His Gospel, must be the weapon in the hand of the missionary toiling in foreign lands, and the beginning and end of all preaching that can ever save or comfort immortal souls. We might shew you how the utter failure of every plan that ever was thought of, for purifying human morals, or elevating human minds, without reference to the work and atonement of Christ, reads like a comment upon our text, as though our Saviour cried aloud to all moralists and philanthropists, "Your purpose indeed is good; but you are taking the wrong way to bring it about: for without Me ye can do nothing!" We might remind you of the memorable confession of one of the most illustrious of Scottish divines, that for twelve years he preached morality without preaching Christ, and that all that time his preaching (eloquent and vehement as it was) had not the weight of a feather upon the moral habits of his parishioners: and that at length he learned that to preach Christ crucified and a sanctifying Spirit was the single way in which men's hearts might be purified and their conduct improved; and that "without Christ he could do nothing!" But we have not time to follow up these tracks of thought which I have thus indicated: and without pursuing them, let us, before we conclude, lead your thoughts to one point in the history of all of us, in which, above all others, we cannot do without Christ.

It is when we come to die. And very awful, my friends, it is to me, when thus on a quiet day of ordinary life, I remember that even now the hour is on the wing, that shall bid this heart cease from its long beating ;—when I remember that somewhere,—but where I cannot tell,—there is a little corner of the world that is "appointed" to be my grave. The tree is grown that shall yield to each of these warm living forms its last "narrow house and dark." I know well, indeed, how on the page of inspiration, and in the writings of fallible men, alike we find much mention of the peace in which the Christian dies. By a peculiar emphasis, "the end of that man *is* peace :" and many besides Balaam, who cared little for living the life of the righteous, have joined in his wish that like the righteous they might die. Every instance in nature that seems to betoken gentle decay, and pensive rather than painful parting, has been taken as the type of the Christian's waning life, and dawning immortality. The fading light of a summer evening, that with all of stillness, and sweetness, and repose, melts away in the western horizon, so that we scarce can see it going, till we look and it is gone : the weary, worn-out winds, that expire so softly, scarcely stirring the lightest leaf as they sink away ; the bright stars, that looked down all night long upon the sleeping world, till in the rosy dawn their beams grew pale, and they died in daylight : —all these have typed the gentle going of the parting breath, the tranquil ebbing of the tide of life, the peaceful severance from this troublesome world. And yet, with all this, it remains a very solemn and awful thing to die. Do you not know this, even you who have seen death come in his least repulsive form,—mothers, who have seen the little eyes close upon this world, and the busy hands folded over the pulseless heart! It is not merely the pain, the weariness, the terrible sinking of heart and strength, that each of us will most probably feel then ;—though no one who knows anything about death as it is will ever speak lightly of even these things about it : it is rather the solemn feeling that we have fairly done with the world we have known so long,—that "this is the last of earth,"—that we are to part for ever from everything we knew and valued here, and to enter "that undiscovered country, from whose bourne no traveller returns,"—to launch away into an untried, unknown state of being, a naked, solitary, shrinking soul ! Kind friends may bear us company to eternity's threshold, but *there* they must leave us, and we must go on alone. The little child, that when the dark shadow fell upon it, thought it was the night that had so often composed it to gentle slumber with a mother bending over it, and whose last little words were Good-night, Good-night, mother,—would waken up on that distant shore alone for the first time in its short life, with no kind mother near. I have often thought, as I have stood by the bed of the dying, how different all earthly things must look to *them*, from what they appear to us in our days of health and strength : how perfectly insignificant many a thing must seem, to which *now* we are ready to attach great importance,—all such things as worldly wealth, and position, and reputation : and I have thought *then* that if it were not for Christ, and for the consolations and hopes of His gospel, it would indeed be a tremendously awful thing to die! Men may fancy that they can do without Christ, perhaps, while they are in the bustle of their life,—when they can be interested in life's business, and enjoy life's comforts and pleasures : but oh! what is business, what is pleasure, to a poor human being that has only an hour to live ;—how intensely such a one must feel that if he has not religion to support him, he has nothing to support him at all! I cannot, by any words I can think of, express to you what I have sometimes felt, of the utter destitution of the soul that is dying without Christ. It has got absolutely *nothing* to rest upon : It can do absolutely *nothing!* If it be not too much stupified and overwhelmed to feel anything distinctly, its feeling must be one of sheer blank unrelieved despair! Oh! I can imagine the monarch, dying without Christ, feeling that he would too thankfully give his empire for another week of bare life : I can imagine the man of vast wealth, dying without Christ, feeling that gladly, gladly would he purchase a month or a week of time to make his peace with God, though he should leave himself a beggar! The hour of death is the time, of all our time on earth, in which we feel it most deeply, that "without Christ we can do **nothing**." Without Him "we dare **not die!**" I do not think it right to appal you by even recalling to your minds the fearful mental agonies in which men have died without Christ: and I would be far from saying that even the best and most devoted believer is sure to find the last parting painless :—sure to go over the dark Jordan dry-shod. I know that many things, spiritual and physical, may tend to throw deep **gloom over the Christian's** dying hour : **but then** this gloom, **if it** be at all, **comes just** because the trembling soul fears it is "without Christ," **or because Christ's presence** is temporarily withdrawn : and we all know in what peace and humble **hope,**— yea in what assurance of salvation and what triumph,— those have passed away from this world who **felt that** their Saviour was near them in their dying **hour. It** would be easy and pleasant to multiply **the histories** of those who have testified that "the sting **of death"** was gone,—that "**the bitterness of death was past,"**— that their Saviour "**had** abolished **death!"** I might remind you of one who when asked, **even in the act** of death, how the dark valley seemed **to her as she** was passing through it, answered "Christ **is here, and** it is *not* dark." God grant, my friends, that when we shall come to that most solemn hour **of all our life,** our Redeemer's gracious presence may **be with us** then! We can have no one else **for a** companion through that solemn way : **O may we** have **Him!** Only the Saviour's presence, that "**Sun of the soul,**" can make sure that "at the evening time there shall be light." And so, like one long ago, "though we walk through the valley of the shadow of death, we shall fear no evil; if Thou art with us, if Thy rod and staff shall comfort us!"

Thus, then, my hearers, we have regarded in several lights, the words of Him who said without arrogance or presumption what never man could say, —"Without Me ye can do nothing." He said it truly. Without Him we can do nothing towards life's first grand work, the working out of our salvation: without Him we can do no good: without Him we can derive no comfort or advantage from the ordinances of religion: without Him day by day we cannot live: without Him we cannot die. We have all got friends without whom we cannot do well: there is just one best Friend without whom we cannot do at all. We avow it: we do not hesitate to express our absolute dependence on Him: we say to Him now, as one of old, "If Thy presence go not with us, carry us not up hence!" No experience of life,—no months of absence,—no other help,—no other things to think of,—will ever enable us to do without Thee! It is an old thing to say that this is a world of partings: and that we are sometimes called to do our best without things and persons, without whom we find it very hard to do. We have all of us learned, perhaps, what it is to turn our back upon the church where we loved to worship,—upon the home where we once were young,—upon the parents whose kind direction we miss at every hour : and yet, though the sunshine may hardly look so bright to us since, we know that such things can be borne. I can imagine,—we have all had opportunities in our lives that may help us in imagining,—how the youth who has had to go out from his quiet home, like a bird from the nest, to push his way in the great world,—away, perhaps, across the Atlantic, with thousands of miles between him and all he loves :—I can imagine well how he felt that parting from home like a tearing away from life ; and how in the first days of absence, as he remembers his mother's sad face and faltering voice as she bade her son farewell, he may feel fit for nothing : he may fancy that away from those dear ones who are thinking of him at home he never can go on in the dreary routine of life,—that "without *them* he can do nothing !" But after a while, in the bustle of his new life, these morbid feelings depart : he toils away industriously,— even cheerfully,—and though he often remembers the fireside he left, he feels that it *is* possible, after all, to live away from it. It gives him a motive to work ; and he labours the harder that he may the sooner go back to gladden the dear hearts there : and to make some little return to a father and a mother for all they did for him. And even when there is no prospect of meeting again in this world, we *can* bear to part from those linked by the closest ties. It is bitter, bitter ;

but still it has been done : it is done every day. What
home of all our homes has not parted with its best and
best-loved one : what family has not lost its purest and
sweetest member : what fireside is there, " howsoe'er
defended, but has one vacant chair !" And yet the
brothers, the sisters, the parents, go about their duties
as usual ; and to the careless world look much as before. Ah, that world does not know that now in that
home, there are doors that are never unlocked, books
that are never looked into, thresholds that are crossed
no more ! Still, we can, sooner or later, in some way or
other, do without every one from whom we can ever be
called to part. Thanks be to God that we need never,
—never at any moment, never anywhere,—part from
that One best and kindest Friend " without whom we
can do nothing !" " Without Me," He says, " ye can
do nothing :" sad, sad words if without Him we ever
needed to be : but He can be " with us" in spite of all
external parting: "Lo," He says, "I am *with you* alway,
even to the end of the world !" Blessed Saviour, fulfil
that gracious promise to our hearts : Go with us where
we go, and dwell with us where we dwell ! We never
know what we can bear till we are tried : we do not
know what endurance there is in these hearts : yet we
know that we can bear all partings else, but not that
last hopeless destitution which lies in being abandoned
by Thee !

VII.

THE PROSPECT PAINFUL YET SALUTARY.

"And **my sin is** ever before **me**."—PSALM li. 3.

IS *that* our way, my friends? Is *that* the prospect that is ever before our eyes and minds? Do we train ourselves to think habitually of our faults; our unworthiness; the foolish things we have often said; the hasty, silly, ill-set, conceited, false, unjust, sinful things we have often done? Or would it not be nearer the truth, in the case of many a man, if he were to say, My merits are ever before me? Many a man is constantly thinking of his good qualities, and his praiseworthy doings: thinking how clever, and wise, and skilful, and judicious, and good he is; and what great things he has done. And instead of taking the text for his own, and saying " My sin is ever before me ;" he would speak the truth if he were to say, " My eminent abilities and deservings are ever before me ; and it shall not be my fault if I do not bring them conspicuously before my fellow-men." And hence it comes, that men are sometimes disappointed and discontented because other people will not recognise their merits and good qualities as they

think they ought : and because they are not advanced
to places of greater distinction and advantage than
they are ever likely to be. There are persons who
not merely have **their** own claims and excellences
and services continually before them, but keep making comparisons between their own, and **the** doings
and deservings **of** their neighbours,—more especially
of those in their own walk of life ;—comparisons very
much in their own favour. And hence come discon-
tent, ingratitude for the many blessings they have,
envying and grieving at a neighbour's good or suc-
cess ; and undutiful murmuring against the appoint-
ments of God's providence. Hence comes, too, a
self-sufficient spirit, far removed from the humble-
mindedness of the true Christian : a disposition to be
pleased with **one's-self, and to** forget what poor help-
less sinners we all are in the sight of God. **Yes, my
friends : all this evil,** and more, comes of our looking
in only one of the two great directions in which man
may look, as regards his own doings and deservings.
It comes of our forgetting the wise counsel to us all,
which is conveyed in this text, **in which** the Psalmist
tells us of something which he was wont to do. **Ah,
he looked at the** other side of the page ! **He** looked
to see how the account stood against him, as well as
how it stood **for** him ! He looked back over his past
life ; and he did **not see much** on which he could
look with entire satisfaction. **He** looked away, over
those departed years ; from the day when he was a

little boy in his father's house and about the sheep, down to the day then present with him on which he was an anointed king. He saw many blessings, many deliverances, many labours, many cares: but there was one dark figure that kept always intruding itself, look where he might, which he knew only too well. There was one reproachful face, one warning and threatening hand,—always there! I sometimes think, he seems to say,—I sometimes think of my doings, my cares, my toils; but there is one thing I never can forget: " My *sin* is ever before me!"

Ah, my brethren, if it were with us, more as it was with David: if we bethought ourselves, oftentimes, of our sins, our failings, our mistakes, our ill-deservings, —we should be more humble, more thankful, more content, more earnestly desirous to fly to that Saviour in whom is all sufficiency, and help, and grace! To look back on our past history, would effectually take us down from all high thoughts of ourselves: would keep us lowly: would lead us, in our utter helpless-ness, to the Redeemer's feet!

Here, then, is the subject for our considera-tion to-day. I trust, before we have done, we may all feel its practical importance. I have no doubt, that most of us have our habits of thinking: have tracks, beaten paths (as it were) of thought, into which we naturally fall, when our minds are not directly occupied with something that puts them on

the stretch. And I have no doubt, too, that each of
us is to himself a subject of such thought to a far
greater degree than is desirable. It is a great thing
to go out of ourselves ; to get clear of the grosser
atmosphere of our own little cares and vexations and
fears : the mind grows very petty and small when it
never ranges beyond the mere daily life and its
worries : and doubtless one great end served by
worthy books, is, that they lift us up above our own-
selves to larger and wider things, and expand the
range of our sympathies. You will think of the true
words of a great poet :

> The man whose eye
> Is ever on himself, doth look on one,
> The least of Nature's works ;—one that might move
> The wise man to that scorn which wisdom holds
> Unlawful ever.

And if we must, by the make of our being, each
feel that his own history is to him the most important
of all histories, and his own concerns more important
than all the other interests of the world together,—
still, any evil effect upon our moral and spiritual
being, of allowing our minds in vacant seasons to fall
too habitually upon the one topic, will be corrected,
—will be turned to blessing,—if we take the advice
implied in the words of the text. Let us, as we think
of ourselves, and of how it has fared with us on our
earthly pilgrimage, not dwell so much on toils that
ended in nothing, on hopes that were disappointed,

on merits little recognised and poorly rewarded,—as we are so prone to do. Let us look in another direction quite : one in which it is not so pleasant to look : one in which many men quite forget to look at all. Let us think how little we have deserved. Let us think how justly God might visit us in wrath. Oh, it will profit us and mend us in many ways, to have our sin ever before us !

And before going on to point out some of these ways, in which it will have a good effect on our spiritual state to train ourselves to a habitual remembrance of our unworthiness and ill-deserving; let me shew you that I am not building upon the text more than it will bear : that I am not snapping a decision in favour of the view I am to set out, from an isolated text of scripture, that by inference, and perhaps by accident, appears to support it. There are many things in Holy Scripture which teach us that however natural it may be, it is not a Christian disposition to be dwelling on our good doings and deservings. You remember the memorable words of Christ,—such words as never were spoken by any human teacher or leader : "Ye, when ye shall have done all those things which are commanded you, say, We are unprofitable servants ; we have done that which it was our duty to do." *There* is the reflection for us, after we have done our best : after we have done much more than we are ever likely to do. You remember, too, the spirit in which we are to work out our salvation. It is anything rather than a self-complacent and confident spirit : it is a humble and anxious one. a spirit deeply convinced of sin and ill-deserving : "Work out your own salvation with fear and trembling !" A habit of daily repentance is the right thing for us : we should every day be going anew to be washed in the fountain opened for sin and uncleanness : in every prayer, whatever else we ask or omit, we must ask for pardon through Christ, and for the Blessed Spirit to sanctify : because we have our "sin ever before us" when we come to the throne of grace. And it is not in the self-satisfied man, accustomed to think how good and deserving he is, that the primary grace of penitence and humility is likely to be found. Some may say, Is there not a conspicuous example of a good man who had his claims and merits a good deal in mind, and who sometimes set them out before his hearers and readers? Did not St Paul sometimes tell of his labours and sufferings, and of the things he had "whereof he might trust in the flesh?" Yes : he sometimes did : but it was always to the end of benefiting others, not of magnifying himself : and even when for this purpose he spoke of his doings and deservings, we find him ever and anon checking himself,—apologising for dwelling on these things at all : saying that he was "a fool in glorying ;" and declaring that as the chief of sinners he looked for salvation simply through Christ. "Of myself," he says, "I will not glory, but in mine infirmities." And you know, my friends, that it is just the best and most Christian people who sincerely speak of themselves as the most unworthy; and as feeling most deeply that only through the Saviour's atonement can they bear God's eye upon them. It is "clothed with humility," that we must present ourselves before God. "Not in mine innocence I trust:" but "this is a faithful saying, and worthy of all acceptation; that Jesus Christ came into the world to save sinners!"

And now, my friends, let us think what good we may get, through doing as David did; and having our sins ever before us. There is no doubt, the view is not a pleasant one. There is hardly anything that men like less, than to be reminded by another of their sins,—unless indeed it be in very general terms, which do not really touch the conscience. Yet things which are painful, are sometimes profitable: and assuredly it is so here.

First, it will make us humble, to think habitually of the many foolish and wrong things we have done. There is a multitude of things which every human being has said and done, on which he cannot look back but with shame and confusion and humiliation. There is a multitude of things which every human being, who is possessed of average sense and conscience, would give a great deal to efface from the remembrance of others, and from his own. It is painful for any one to plainly see, that on a certain occasion he acted like a fool : but it is far more painful and more humbling to have our eyes opened by God's Spirit to the crushing knowledge of our sins ;—to be made to feel, not merely in a general way, that we are sinners, — everybody will confess *that*, readily enough : but to be made to feel that this and that and the other thing actually done, is sin against God,—to be made to feel that this and the other year or years of life cannot in any way be justified,—must be given over, as beyond mending or extenuating, wrong.   Yet, painful as it may be to think of these things : ready and willing as we might all be, instead of having them " ever before us," to banish them from our remembrance for ever ; it is right and fit that we should oftentimes think of them : for there is no doubt whatsoever that it is good for us to be humble ; and there is nothing in this world that will humble us like *that*.   If we would cultivate that grace, essential to the Christian character, of lowliness in the sight of God, here is the way to cultivate it. And if we would avoid that proud and self-righteous spirit, hateful in the sight of God, and so unbecoming our nature and our place, and such a grievous hindrance in the Christian race from its first step to its latest here,—then let us beware of dwelling upon what we fancy our merits : let us beware, when we sit down by the evening fireside in an hour of leisure, or when we go forth for a lonely walk, of getting into the way of running over the story of our life, and thinking of all our hard work, all our wise and good doings; and comparing ourselves with this one and that, who has got on better than we have in the battle of life, without (as we think) having deserved it half so well. There once was a man, who got thoroughly confirmed in the habit of dwelling on his own good deeds and merits; and of comparing himself, much to his own advantage, with other men. And so inveterate grew that habit, that coming to God in prayer, when every mortal should lie as in the very dust of true humility, he could not help summing up his merits even there. And so, upon a certain day, going up to God's house to pray, he offered a prayer which is recorded for our warning. Here it is: "God, I thank thee that I am not as other men are: extortioners, unjust, adulterers, or even as this publican. I fast twice in the week: I give tithes of all that I possess." *That* was his prayer, if indeed you can call it a prayer: and we have no reason to think it contained a word that was not quite true. Very likely he did fast, and give tithes, as he said: very likely he was not an extortioner, nor unjust, nor impure: it is not because his prayer was false, that it was such a bad prayer: it is because it set out his merits, and said not a word about his sins. *His* sins, it is plain, were far from being ever before him. But he was thoroughly up in the catalogue of his good deeds: *they* were before him often enough. There was another man *there* upon the same occasion: I daresay a man who had done many wrong things, and who could have made up but a very poor list of his virtues: yet *that* man, from the depths of a contrite heart, offered a true and good prayer: one which suits us all: one that the great God above us approved and liked, though it was very short, and very simple. But *that* poor man had his sins before him; and was thinking of *them.* If he ever had done anything good in his unworthy life, it was not *then* that he thought of it! He did not say a word about his merits, if he had any: and yet the blessed Redeemer tells us he " went down to his house justified rather than the other!" For he, with his sins before him, " standing afar off, would not lift up so much as his eyes unto heaven; but smote upon his breast, saying, God be merciful to me a sinner!"

My friends, *there* we have fairly put before us, by our Saviour Himself, an example of the practical effect upon a human being, of having his sin before him, and of having his merits before him. You see what it lands a man in, to think much, and to think only, of his deservings: you see what it leads to, to think of our sins. And if the publican's attitude before God was the right one, and the pharisee's the wrong one: if the publican's prayer was the right prayer for every man, and the pharisee's the wrong prayer for any man: oh brethren, as you would cultivate that humble spirit without which the Christian character lacks its very foundation: be cautious how you indulge yourselves in the perilous contemplation of what you may think your good deeds ; and see to it, that your "sin be ever before you !"

There are other good things which come of having our sin ever before us ; which, after all, simply means taking a just view of our doings and character : for sin and imperfection cleave to all we do ; and our great characteristic, as human beings, is, that we are sinners. All these advantageous results of habitual meditation upon our unworthiness are perhaps implied in that primary grace of humility ; yet they grow out of it, and may be distinguished from it.

So let us go on to think, that the habitual contemplation of our sinfulness will .tend to make us thankful to God : to make us contented with our lot : to put down anything like envy in our hearts, at the greater success and eminence of others.   A man who is always thinking of his own merits and services, sees them as much bigger than other people do.   We all know, that it is a natural consequence of considering any subject very much or very long, that it grows greatly in apparent importance.   And so you find people naturally magnify their own vocation, or the special matter to which they give their thoughts.   And we must all have observed, that people who are much given to dwelling on their own doings and deservings, their position, their influence and the like, come to entertain, quite honestly, a

wherever there are sinful human hearts! Perhaps there is some tendency to *that* in every one of us. Even a good and Christian man is sometimes tempted to think, that his merits are not quite recognised as they deserve,—that he has not quite had justice done him, yet: And we can easily see what evil and un-christian feelings are apt to follow :—unthankfulness towards God ;—discontent with our lot ;—envying and grieving at the good of others.

And now, my friends, how to get rid of all these? Oh, look in a different direction. Look to the other side of the account. You have thought of your well-deserving : Now think of your ill-deserving! Your merits have been much before your eye : now let your sins be so! Ah, think, has not God given you far more than you deserve? You know the evil of your own heart: you know the flaws and defects in your best doings, which others do not see! If you have been enlightened at all by God's Spirit to a per-ception of your true condition, then each of you knows how evil you are, better than any one ex-cept God! Look at that weak sinful foolish heart, with its vain fancies and idle thoughts : think how often you have got credit from others, for being far, far better than you knew yourself to be: think of words and deeds without number, that would crush you down with confusion if they were now set out plainly before this congregation here : think of the foolish, ill-set, vain, wicked, indefensible things that

you have said and done : and say, Have you not received at God's hand as much good as you deserve ?
Ought not each one of us to be thankful that we are
in the place of hope ! Where should we be ; and
what should we be ; if God dealt with us according to
our merits ? If people knew you as you know yourself, would they think as well of you as they do ? Oh
brethren, if it were with you, as it was with the
Psalmist : if your sin were ever before you ; surely
you would fling away envy and malice ; you would
learn to be thankful and content !

And now, let us think, in the third place, of something even better and more valuable, as resulting
from having our sin ever before us, than these things
of which we have been thinking ;—although these
things do bear, most weightily and directly, on our
Christian character, and our eternal state. To feel
our sinfulness ;—to have our sins set before us, by
God's Spirit, in such a way that it will be impossible
to help seeing them, and seeing them as bad as they
really are ;—is the thing that will lead us to Christ ;
lead us to true repentance on account of our sins ;
and to a simple trust in Him who " saves His people
from their sins." You know,—every one knows,—
that salvation is to be found only by going to the
Redeemer, and resting upon Him : But the man who
takes the one-sided view of himself and his doings ;—
the man who thinks much of his merits and little of

his sins ;—is not in the frame to go to Christ and say, "Nothing in my hand I bring : simply to Thy Cross I cling !" No one will really feel, whatever he may say, that his own "righteousness is as filthy rags," who has trained himself to think that his own righteousness is really very good, and his own deservings very great. Yet, if we are ever saved through Christ, and by His grace, and God's love in Him, we must get entirely off the ground of our own merits. We must learn to come as helpless sinful creatures, deserving nothing good at God's hand ; our very best deeds unworthy and imperfect ; offending in many things, coming short in all ; to take salvation as the free gift of God. If we are to be striving daily to find the supply of a want, the way is to have that want ever before us and ever pressed home upon us. If we are to be striving daily to be pardoned and sanctified, it must be because we daily see, in our sins, what makes pardon and sanctification the first and most urgent of all our needs. Oh surely it is fit and right, that beings like us, whose main characteristic is that they are sinners, should always be remembering what they are : that beings whose great want is the pardon of sin, should always be feeling that it is so : that beings whose better life cannot be maintained from day to day but by the presence of the Holy Spirit, should live mindful of that truth : And how shall these things be, unless, when thinking of ourselves, we take, not a partial and one-sided, but a full and complete, view of the case, by having, and keeping, " our sin ever before us ! "

There are pleasanter views ; but none more profitable. It is good for us to think of our sins. There is no need to think of our good deeds ;—if indeed we have many to think of: we cannot change *them* now. But to think of our sins, may make a great difference upon *them.* For though the *deed* remains, yet the *sin* may be blotted out by true repentance, and justifying faith. 'To think of our merits, and dwell on them, is a mere piece of selfish gratification : but to think of our sins, and dwell upon them, in a right spirit, may lead to the most precious practical results. Very naturally, after the words which form our text : after " my sin is ever before me : " comes the Psalmist's prayer, " Hide thy face from my sins, and blot out all mine iniquities. Create in me a clean heart, O God ; and renew a right spirit within me." May the like contemplation, my friends, lead each of us to the like earnest prayer !

I cannot but linger upon my text. I thought of it, last Sunday evening : I have been thinking of it very much since ; and thinking how blessed a change it would work upon this world, if we had all more of the spirit to which the text would lead. What humble-minded, kindly, charitable, thankful, contented, Christian people would all men be, if, to good purpose, they kept their " sin ever before" them! It would be all kindliness, and mutual help: no disposition to bear hard on an offending brother: we should be ready to forgive, feeling that we need to have so much forgiven: and never forgetting that we owe ten thousand talents,—having ever before us that great, overwhelming debt we owe to God,—and that never will be paid unless Christ pays it for us,—we should not bear hard upon a poor fellow-sinner who owes us a hundred pence. And never, never, should we designedly do anything to vex or grieve a human being! All loaded with the same weight of sin and sorrow;—all to be saved, if saved at all, by the same atoning blood;—all, in a little while, to pass through the same lowly gate of death, and to sleep in the dust together;—is there one that would say or do the thing that was merely to give pain to another! And oh, looking back over these lives we have led, to this day: thinking of the omissions, the imperfections, the failures,—the sins of heart and thought, of word and deed,—O let us, my fellow-sinners, fly for refuge to the same Blessed One, whose glory is that He " receiveth sinners :" let us bend together at the throne of grace, saying " *Our* Father,— Forgive us our debts, as we forgive our debtors !"

VIII.

DEPARTED TROUBLE AND WELCOME REST.

"There the wicked cease from troubling; and there the weary be at rest."—Job iii. 17.

THE day was, when it was thought a fit thing that the Christian's last resting-place should be surrounded by gloomy and repulsive associations; and when it was thought right that around the grave there should be gathered the sad emblems of mortal decay, rather than the memorials of immortal hope. In the gloom of cathedral vaults, where the sunbeam would never fall nor the daisy grow, the dust was given to the dust from which it came: and the dark fancy of the sculptor ran riot in devising ghastly tokens of the degradation of that which was the human body, now under the dominion of decay and death. It was not of peaceful rest,—not of the glorious deliverance from sin and sorrow,—not of the Saviour's blessed face seen without a veil at last,—that the burying-place of the middle ages would remind you; but rather of mouldering bones and dream·less heads: as though *that* had been most, or all.

And most of us can remember how, in our early days, the churchyard of the parish we knew, was like anything rather than what a Christian burying-place should be made by people who believe that the believer's breathless body is "still united to Christ;" and is waiting for a glorious resurrection. We remember the locked-up, deserted, neglected place, all grown over with great weeds and nettles: and looking not like God's Acre, the holiest place in the parish, but rather like an accursed spot, which no little child would willingly go near. I see something more than improved taste and judgment, in those quiet, beautiful, carefully-tended spots with which we have grown so familiar; and where faces and forms often missed from our firesides, have been laid to their long repose. It is not merely better judgment, but sounder faith, that is here: it is a thoroughly Christian thing, to scatter the beauties of nature around the Christian grave: it is fit and right that *there* flowers should spring up and die, with their silent reminder of death and of resurrection: it is fit and right that the survivor should often visit the place where rests the mortal part of one who though far away, is a member of the family yet, as much as ever: and there, perhaps, remember more vividly than ever elsewhere, His blessed words who said; "I am the resurrection and the life: he that believeth in Me, though he were dead, yet shall he live: And whosoever liveth and believeth in Me, shall never die!"

I see something, my friends, in the most beautiful text to which you have listened, that is like turning the ghastly, neglected, nettle-grown graveyard which we may remember in childhood, into the quiet, sweet, thoughtful sleeping-place which we find so commonly now. Surely very like that pleasant change, is the change which passes upon our conception of our last resting-place, when we think of it not as man has often described and often made it, but as the ancient patriarch Job sets it before us here. I have many times thought of preaching from these memorable words: but I remembered what was said by a great divine as the reason why he had never preached from another very familiar verse of Holy Scripture. He said that really he could only repeat his text, if he were to seek to discourse upon it: that he could add nothing to its force and beauty. Yet let us try to-day, to rest in the contemplation of these words we all know so well; and which, in many a time of weariness and trouble, have come so welcome to the Christian's heart. There are few words, indeed, that fall more pleasantly upon the ear. How gently, how graciously, amid the fever and the toils of life, our blessed faith seems to take us by the hand, and to point us to a place where all these are done with: saying, "There the wicked cease from troubling; and there the weary are at rest!"

This text speaks to us, over nearly four thousand years. Isaac was but a youth, in the days when Job lived. But the oldest book in the world; this book of Job, has never been surpassed for beauty and sublimity by any of all that came after it : and even it never rose to higher strains than in those verses of which the text is one. Yet we are to remember this : that Job lived in days when the light of truth was dim : the Sun of Righteousness had not yet risen above the horizon : and Jesus had not yet brought life and immortality to light : and thus it is possible that we are able to understand Job's words more fully and better than he understood them himself. The text may be read, first, as of the grave : but in its best meaning, it speaks of a better world, to which the grave is the portal. Now, many of you know, that while all are agreed in believing that a future life was not revealed to Job as plainly as it is revealed to us, some have maintained that Job had no knowledge of a life beyond the grave at all : and so, that in the text he speaks not merely of the grave first, but of the grave only. It is not needful now to discuss the question as to Job's knowledge ; which has been discussed already not only very much, but very bitterly. It is plain that *we* are entitled to read those verses in the light of present revelation : and after looking at the text in the sense which it first bears, we shall go on to its completion in a farther and a higher.

Let us think, then, first, of these words, as spoken of the grave ; which, as you know, Job elsewhere calls "the house appointed for all living."

It is not needful that we should seek to justify the impatient burst, in which Job wished, as many others have wished since, that he had never been born. You will think of a great man in former days, who regularly as his birth-day came round, thought he could not better observe it, than by reading by himself this chapter of the book of Job. Jonathan Swift, a Christian divine and a great deal more, in the review of a wasted and disappointed life, took up the ancient story of the patient patriarch in his impatient day: and many a one beside, in the bitter conviction that all life has proved a failure, has done the like. You remember how trouble after trouble came upon that home in the land of Uz: how first the patriarch's worldly wealth was taken: then all his children were reft away together: then loathsome bodily anguish laid upon himself: how his three friends came to comfort him, and when they saw him did not know him, so changed was he in that little time. Not a word had they of consolation: the easy commonplaces with which the cheerful and well-to-do commonly condole with the suffering, would not do in a case so extreme as that. And it was after seven gloomy days of silence, that Job broke forth into this passionate, desolate cry, wishing the day of his birth had never been. He had not our gospel light, nor our strong consolation: the Blessed Spirit of all comfort was not known to Job as He is known to us: yet of course Job's impatience is a thing that cannot be fully justified;

though it would be interesting to see the human being that feels entitled to cast a stone at him. After that first outbreak of wretched feeling, the patriarch calms a little down : and then he comes to that beautiful description of the rest into which he would have gone, if he had been spared the toil and the trouble here. He tells us how he would have slumbered, with the great, the wise, and the good : how he would have lain still and been quiet, where trouble could never come, in the peaceful grave.

And there, he says, for one pleasant thing, "the wicked cease from troubling." Yes : there is one place into which the suffering can escape, where their persecutors have no power. Cross the line, that parts life from death ; and the strongest human hand cannot reach to vex or harm, any more. There have been striking examples, that bring this home to us strongly. We have all heard the story of that Highland soldier, who fell, in war, into the hands of a savage Indian tribe. The Indians were preparing, according to their barbarous custom, to put their prisoner to death by horrible lingering tortures. You remember how he evaded these. He told his captors, that he possessed a magic charm which rendered him invulnerable : and, for proof of this, he bade one of the strongest warriors among the Indians to take a sword and try to cut off his head ; saying that the savage, striking with all his force, could not inflict so much as a scratch upon him. Scarcely were the words said, when the savage, fetching a tremendous blow, made the soldier's head fly for many yards from his body. And then, the barbarians felt that they were foiled and befooled; the brave Highlander was gone where they could not reach to torture! There is no more touching instance of this escape, suggesting itself so naturally to the mind, than occurred in one of those outbursts in the Indian Mutiny, when it seemed as if all hell had broken loose. You know how a brave Scotchman, with his young wife, was in a tower that was attacked by a great force of those incarnate devils: you know how, in the last extremity, when all hope was gone, he found, in death, for him and his, a retreat where the wicked could trouble no more. And you will think of the blood-thirsty Roman Emperor, who, hearing that an enemy whom he designed for torture was dead, exclaimed in bitterness, "Ah, has that man escaped me!" And indeed he *had* escaped him, thoroughly and completely. There is nothing more striking about the state of those who have gone into the unseen world, than the completeness of their escape from all worldly enemies, however malignant, and however powerful. And it is so with all the troubles of this mortal life, small and great. All the cares of life, all its anxieties, all its pains and bereavements, are cast off utterly when you pass the line into the state of the departed. "There the wicked cease from troubling:" cease, absolutely and completely, and for evermore!

But there is something beyond the mere escape from

worldly evil. Now, the busy heart is quiet at last, and the weary head lies still. "There," says Job, "the weary are at rest." "The weary?" and oh, what a multitude is numbered of *them!* Not merely those who often feel the daily weariness growing on the over-driven body and mind: all are weary, more or less; and grow more so as they go on. Oh brethren, if all were right beyond, how many would be thankful to lay the jaded body down to rest; and to cease from the weary round! Many a human being has said sincerely, in the time of weariness and trouble, "I wish I was in my grave!" Often hastily said, foolishly said, and not quite sincerely said, the words yet testify to a longing, sometimes felt, to creep to that dreamless rest of forgetfulness, and (like Job) to "lie still!" And though humbly submissive to God's good will; and though feeling that "to live is Christ:" and though aware that to abide here is needful for others' sake: yet the best of the race have sometimes known what it is to look forward with a sigh to that perfect calm: wherein we think, with a kind of confused feeling, that morning after morning the rising to toil and care will cease: where will be no anxious calculations how to make the most of the little store, which barely yields bread to eat and raiment to put on. It is oftentimes comforting; and we cannot say it is not sometimes fit and right; to think of a place where we shall find peace and quiet: where "the weary are at rest."

But though a deep sleep fall upon the body, it is only for a while. And indeed, after all, there is a certain delusion in thinking of the grave as a place of quiet rest. The soul lives still, and is awake and conscious, though the body sleeps : and it is our souls that are ourselves. We cannot throw *them* off : nor escape conscious life. Each of us lives, and must live, for ever : and we have no warrant for believing that in the other world there will be any season of unconsciousness to the soul. But now our subject calls us rather to think that even *that* in us which does sleep,—even the body,—sleeps to wake again. Let us ever remember, as we look at a Christian burying-place, that it is only a place of sleep. It is striking to think, in that silent and solitary place, of the great stir and bustle there shall be in it some day ! There they have been perhaps for centuries,—the little grassy undulations, and the green mossy stones. But " the hour is coming," which shall make a total change. This quiet, this decay, this forgetfulness, are not to last ! It has been doubted whether Job knew all the reach of meaning there is in his words, when he uttered those memorable ones whose force *we* understand so well. " For I know that my Redeemer liveth : and that he shall stand at the latter day upon the earth : and though after my skin worms destroy this body, yet in my flesh shall I see God ! "

But now, my friends, let us go on to something

farther and better. There is no doubt, that when Job uttered these words of the text, he was thinking first, if he was not thinking only, of the quiet grave. But though these are Old Testament words, we read them by New Testament light: as those who know that Jesus is the Resurrection and the Life to all His people. We take the words in their higher and truer meaning. We know where it is, that in the best and noblest sense, " the wicked cease from troubling, and the weary are at rest."

These words speak of a better world. They point us onward to heaven. And let us mark what are the two great things they tell us of that glorious and happy place. The two great things of which they assure us, and remind us, are Safety; and Peace. There are many things about that blessed life and world which our Redeemer purchased for us by His life and death, which we do not know nor understand; and which, as we are, we could not understand nor know. But these two grand characteristics of the life and immortality brought to light by our Saviour, we can, in some measure, comprehend, even now, and here.

First, there is to be safety, and the sense of safety. " There the wicked cease from troubling." Not wicked men only ; but everything wicked : evil spirits, evil thoughts, evil influences, our own sinful hearts. All danger, all temptation, shall trouble us no more. Everything evil, whether within us or around us, shall be done with. And who that can think at all but knows, that if evil were gone, trouble would go too! Where the *wicked* cease from troubling, there will be no trouble at all. Not the kind angelic companions: not the happy souls met again never to part: not the pure soul itself, "made perfect in holiness:" none of these will trouble or vex. There never will be a cloud to obscure the Saviour's face: never an uneasy doubt: never a perplexing fear. There never will be an unkind word: never an unfriendly look: never an uncharitable interpretation of what was meant sincerely and well. There will be no *trouble* of any kind or degree. Now, brethren, we hear it said commonly enough, that the thing we can best understand about the better world, is rather the evil that shall be absent, than the holiness and happiness which shall be present. And in one sense, doubtless, *that* is true. The bliss of the redeemed can never be rightly understood till it is felt. But it is very nearly as hard for us to understand a state in which evil and trouble shall be entirely absent. Our whole life here is so much made up of trouble: we have so much of evil, so much of care, temptation, worry, always about us: that our imagination fails us when we seek to realise what life would be with these away. And then, the great thing about evil and trouble is not so much the pain and suffering they cause us; as the terrible power they have, unless specially sanctified by the Holy Spirit, to do us fearful spiritual harm. It is not merely that here the wicked may trouble us: not merely that wicked angels, wicked men, wicked influences from the wicked world around us, wicked feelings and impulses in our **own** sinful natures, may trouble us in the sense of destroying our peace and causing us distress : but that all these things may lead us quite away from God ; may quench in us those influences of the Blessed Spirit that should bring us to the Saviour, and make us one with Him. In this world, we are always on the enemy's ground : we breathe an unfriendly atmosphere : there are a thousand influences ever bearing upon us that tend to make us worldly and ungodly. But in that happy home for which we look, all these are over. *There*, for the first time in all the believer's life, he can feel perfectly safe. There will be no need to be ever "taking heed lest he fall :" no need to combine watchfulness against the insidious approaches of temptation, with the glorious praises there ! Across the boundary of that better country which we seek, evil can never come : for "there the wicked,"—all that is wicked,—"anything that defileth,"—"shall cease from troubling,"—shall cease utterly, and cease for evermore !

But there is more. There is many a poor, vexed, troubled, overdriven being in this world, who would be too thankful only to be saved from all trouble : to think that he would never be worried any more. But besides the negative assurance, that trouble will be done with in Heaven, we have the promise of a positive blessing. "There the weary are at rest." You need hardly be reminded by what common consent the happiness and peace of the better world are summed up in that word. You know by what common consent of the thoughtful even among such as enjoyed no revelation, rest was taken to be man's greatest blessing and good. "The end of work," said one of the wisest of heathens, "is to enjoy rest." And you will remember how the wearied Psalmist summed all he wanted in that word. "Oh that I had wings like a dove! then would I fly away and be at rest." And as if to answer and meet the blind gropings of humanity, come the blessed Saviour's words of invitation and promise: "Come unto Me, all ye that labour and are heavy laden; and I will give you rest." You know, too, how the apostle says in a word what holiness and happiness await the Christian beyond the grave: "There remaineth a rest for the people of God." And you know, likewise, what the "voice from heaven" said in the hearing of St John: "Blessed are the dead which die in the Lord from henceforth: Yea, saith the Spirit, that they may rest from their labours."

And so it is, my friends, that in the heaven into which we hope through our blessed Lord some day to enter, we shall find nothing better than rest. But oh what a large, all-comprehending blessing; and what a rest it will be! *There*, at last, the thirsty soul that never was satisfied in this world will be fully content: and there will be no more of the care-worn, anxious, weary faces, that here seem to look at you earnestly, and with a vague inquiry for something,— the something that is lacking in all things here. And we know the meaning of all the vague and endless aspirations of our human hearts. It is that "this is not our rest:" our rest is beyond the grave. It is idle to try to sum up the items that go to make an immortal soul happy. Doubtless there will be rest from sin, from sorrow, from toil, from anxiety, from temptation, from pain: but all *that* fails to convey the whole unspeakable truth: it will be the beatific presence of the Saviour that will make the weary soul feel it never knew rest before! There is a something of life's fitful fever about all the bliss of this life: but in that world the bliss will be restful: calm, satisfied, self-possessed, sublime. It will be "the peace of God, which passeth all understanding." Only in Him, as seen in our beloved Saviour's face, is the rest and consummation of an immortal soul. You remember the Psalmist's words, so devoutly earnest, so calmly sensible: "Whom have I in heaven but Thee; and there is none upon earth that I desire beside Thee!" And you remember words, meet to be set beside them: "Thou madest us for Thyself; and our souls are restless till they find rest in Thee!"

O think who gives that rest which can make us happy; and to whom He gives it. The only rest that ever truly and permanently quieted the human heart is that which the Saviour gives,—*His* peace, not as the world giveth! And He gives it only to His own: that is, to all who will humbly take it. Is there one sinful, heavy-laden creature here that will refuse the peace He bought for us with His blood? It is not the quiet grave into which the weary and anxious have often wished they could creep and lie still;—not *that* which can soothe away our fears. Only He can give it, whose word never fails; and whose promise to the weary who will come to Him, is, "I will give you rest!"

And as we draw these thoughts to a close, we look again upon that text. There it is, as we remember it since we can remember anything: the same to us as it has been to generations of human beings for six and thirty hundred years; with its promise of departed trouble, and of ever welcome rest. But whensoever we recall those words, to ourselves or to others, oh let us read them by gospel light,—let us read them in the beams of the Sun of Righteousness! Let us never forget which is the satisfying rest; and where it is that the text holds true. Let us lay the dead in places so quiet and sweet, as shall beseem the body's long repose: where country streams murmur by with their gentle requiem, and ancient trees shed their leaves upon the grave: or by the pleasant shore, as the poet tells us, and in the hearing of the sea: but let us never be so false to Him who is the Resurrection and the Life, as to fancy that it is *there* the text is fulfilled. Nay: but when we would look towards the place of which the Patriarch's words are truest, let us turn our eyes not to the green earth below, but to the bright heaven above: let us think, not of the senseless slumber in the dust of the poor dying body, but of the bliss and purity and safety of the immortal soul: and looking towards that Golden City,—towards that "Country" sought so earnestly by the "strangers and pilgrims on the earth,"—with its perfect peace, and holiness, and happiness,—let us thank God that " *There*," indeed,— that " *There*, the wicked cease from troubling; and the weary are at rest !"

IX

CONTINUANCE THE TEST OF RELIGIOUS PROFESSION.

"And that your fruit should remain."—JOHN xv. 16.

THERE are few things which, as we grow older and get more experience, impress us more deeply, than the transitoriness of thoughts and feelings in the human heart.   We observe this in those around us; and we feel this in ourselves.   Places and persons that we once thought we never could forget, as years go on are all but quite forgotten: and feelings that we once thought would have remained in our hearts so long as they beat, as years go on, come to stir their pulses no more.   Some of us may remember the days when we fancied we never could be happy away from the home of our youth, and the pang with which we left it: but now, perhaps, we never miss it though it has not been seen for years.   Some of us may remember with what sorrow we left the scene and the friends of some happy period of our life, which now, away in the past, looks faint and far.   They leave their trace indeed, these strong feelings of the heart: their faded relics may sometimes be awakened to life again : they do not leave us exactly what we were ;—but still they leave us.

And there is no respect in which this is more sadly felt, than in the case of pious feelings and holy resolutions. We can yet remember, perhaps, the warm and happy emotions of Communion seasons long ago : the eagerness of our first choice of Christ as our souls' portion : the warm and confident resolutions which we thought would never yield, that hereafter we should give ourselves entirely to Him ; and it seemed easy then to renounce the world, to set the affections on things above : and life, which is really a long thing, with great power to wear down the keenest feelings and the strongest resolutions, seemed in that early flush only the short passage and portal to Eternity. We say nothing now as to whose fault it is, or whether it be anybody's fault, that it is so : but surely in the case of many the cold hearts of to-day contrast sadly with those hours of sacred elevation; and the growing worldliness of spirit which we feel it so hard to keep down, is not like that early choice of heaven and of immortality. We often think sadly of those whose goodness was like the morning cloud and the early dew, which soon pass away. We sometimes fear lest we have been deluding ourselves with the belief that we were better and safer than we ever have been : and mourn for the soul-refreshing views, the earnest purpose, the warm affections, of the days when we first believed in Christ.

Now there is no doubt, that it is possible to carry such reflections too far. No doubt, by the make of our being, as we grow older, we grow less capable of emotion ; and our choice of Christ may be just as strong, and our religious convictions as deep, though they less frequently than once thrill the heart, and stir the depths of feeling. Religion in the soul, after all, is a matter of fixed choice and resolution,—of principle rather than of feeling : and it would be very wrong if any old believer thought, that because he now no longer feels so deeply, perhaps, on a Communion Sunday, he is therefore falling away from the attainments of former years. It is only with him that the lamp of *all* feeling is burning lower,—that the heart is less easily stirred : but still the choice of heaven may be as fixed, and the faith in Jesus as deep as ever. Do not dishearten and vex yourselves, my believing friends, in trying to awaken emotion which no longer comes. The still, subdued light of the Autumn twilight is as beautiful in its season as the blaze of the summer day. And the calm, thoughtful mood in which the old man covers his face, as he bends over the white cloth, befits as well the calm Feast of Remembrance, as do the young believer's tears.

And yet it remains a great and true principle, that in the matter of Christian faith and feeling, *that* which lasts longest is best. This indeed is true of most things. The worth of anything depends much upon its durability,—upon the wear that is in it. A thing that is merely a fine flash and over, only disappoints It is not one bright hour that makes a fine day: it is the equable continuance of the cheerful light that makes it. It is not the gaudy annual we value most, but the steadfast forest-tree. The slight triumphal-arch, run up in a day, may flout the sober-looking buildings near it; but they remain after it is gone. And our Blessed Saviour, in the text, acknowledges the truth of this great principle. He tells his disciples that they, as branches of Himself, the living Vine, were to bear fruit,—to bring forth *much* fruit : "Herein is my Father glorified, that ye bear much fruit; so shall ye be my disciples." And what is meant by fruit, and much fruit, every one feels at once ; for the analogy between the fruit of a tree and the life and conduct of a man is too plain to need any tracing. But even fruit, and much fruit, was not enough for the Saviour's desire and God's glory. The fairest profession for a time, the most earnest labours for a time, the most ardent affection for a time, would not suffice. And so the Redeemer's words are, mark them well,— "I have chosen you, and ordained you, that ye should go and bring forth fruit ;—and that *your fruit should remain.*"

No doubt, brethren, the disciples to whom Christ addressed these words, had a work to do beyond that which can be allotted to any of us. *They* had to found the Christian Church : and it was a matter of momentous concern, not for God's glory only, but for the sake of a sinful world, that their handy-work should be firm and durable,—that it should *remain* even until the end of time.   But it is not in that special sense in which we wish at present to understand the text.   We wish to understand it just as suggesting the great principle, that in religion, Permanence is the great test.   *That* only is the true fruit of the Spirit, which *remains,*— which does not wear out with advancing time.   The text hints to us, that it is even a harder thing to keep up a consistent Christian profession,—to keep it up year after year, through temptations, through troubles, through the slow wear of time,—than to make it, however fairly, at the first.   Our Christian profession may indeed lose something of its gloss,—may get somewhat battered and travel-stained as we go on our pilgrimage-path : but still, in the main,—in all that makes its essence, it must go on with us. We are to see to it that we bring forth fruit,—"and that our fruit should remain."

And our first remark upon this precept is this : that it is only by our fruit remaining that we are warranted in believing that it is the right fruit. The only satisfactory proof either to ourselves or to those around us that our Christian faith, and hope, and charity, are the true fruits of the Spirit, is, that they shall last,— that they shall stand the wear of advancing time.   In religion, it is not merely that the fruit which "remains" is the best fruit : the fruit which "remains" is the only fruit.   Anything else is a false pretender. Continuance is the test of Christian grace being genuine. And herein is a point of difference between worldly and spiritual things. We have said that most things in this world are valuable in proportion to their durability: but it would not be just to say that things which wear out, and even wear out fast, have no value at all. Who shall say that the flower which blooms in the morning and withers before the sunset, is not a fair and kind gift of the Creator: who shall affirm that the summer sunset is not beautiful, though even while we gaze upon it, its hues are fading? Who shall deny that there is something precious in the lightsome glee of childhood, even though in a little while that cheerful face is sure to be shadowed by the cares of manhood? Indeed it has been maintained that the beauty and value of many things in this world are increased by the shortness of the time for which they last: that many things borrow a charm from their very evanescence: and that no one feels so keenly the beauty of the fairest landscape, as the dying man who knows that he is very soon to look upon it no more. But it is not thus with Christian grace. If it be not a grace which will last for ever, it is no grace at all. If it be not worth everything, it is worth nothing. Ah brethren, a man may shew every appearance of being a true disciple: his convictions of sin may be deep, his sense of the Saviour's needfulness strong, his zeal in all Christian exercises great: he may read his Bible carefully, he may pray often and much, he may never be out of God's house, he may be deeply impressed at a Communion-table, he may be eager to do good to all as he has opportunity: and all these things are well: but oh! if they last but for a little, if the zeal wanes and expires, if the throne of grace is deserted, and the Bible no longer read, and the little task of Christian philanthropy abandoned: how much reason there is then to fear lest the man was deceiving himself with a name to live while he was dead,—that he was mistaking the transient warmth of mere human emotion for the gracious working of the Holy Spirit of God! God forbid that we should judge any man: and we know that even they whose names are written in the Lamb's book of Life, who are effectually called and sanctified, and so who can never totally and finally fall from grace and end in woe, may yet fall into grievous sin, and continue therein for a time: but, though we should ever be charitable when we judge our neighbour, it is wisdom to be severe when we judge ourselves: and brethren, how *can* we but fear and tremble when we feel grace within decaying and weakening, lest our fruit should not be that fruit which shall remain,—lest our profession should prove a delusion which deceived even ourselves! It *may* be otherwise: our flagging zeal and our chilling heart may be the signs only of the temporary intermission of the true grace, and not of the final failure of the false: but who shall set his eternal destiny upon that fearful chance,—who shall not rather set himself to earnest prayer, and stir himself up to vigorous effort, to "strengthen the things which remain, which are ready to die?" The doctrine of what is called the *Perseverance of the Saints*, when rightly regarded, so far from tending to make men spiritually indolent,— to make them cease from the diligent use of the means of grace, and rest in the confidence that having once been right, they never can go wrong,—is a doctrine which should tend in the very reverse direction,—which should stir men up to ceaseless prayer and endeavour, and which should make them trem. blingly watchful of the faintest symptom of spiritual declension, lest *that* should be the indication that their profession of religion is a delusion, and that they have never yet gone to Christ at all. Who should be so fearful of the least appearance of going wrong, as he who believes that to go wrong is an indication which makes it fearfully likely that he has never been right? And it is sad to think how this great doctrine, which ought to stimulate to constant exertion to keep the armour bright and the profession unsullied, has been used or abused to just the opposite end. We read in history that when a certain man who had filled a high place in this world was dying, he was filled with many fears and forebodings as to how he stood with God. He sent for his spiritual advisers, and anxiously asked of them whether it were possible for the elect to fall finally: and being answered in the negative, replied, "Then I am safe; for I am certain that I *was once* in a state of grace." And so, instead of turning even then to the Saviour, who is ready to receive and pardon even to the eleventh hour, the dying man drugged his soul with that delusive opiate; which if it meant anything, just meant this pernicious and false idea, that "if a man has been at any time satisfied, from his own feelings, of being in a state of grace, he will infallibly be saved, and is not to regard any sin or course of sin, he may subsequently fall into, as endangering his final acceptance." Ah brethren, by far the more natural and likely interpretation of the fact that a professing Christian has fallen into grievous sin, or has even chilled down into utter heartlessness and heedlessness, is, that his profession was unsound. The man who feels that he is now far wrong, has weighty reason for fearing that he never was right at all. For *that* only is the right fruit, which *remains:* that only is the true grace, which stands the wear of years. And when we remember how ready we are to deceive ourselves, and to pass sentence unjustly in our own favour, oh with what caution we should receive any testimony borne, as we may fancy, by our own soul to our own soul's state! Yea, how decidedly we should reject that self-borne testimony, if we know that now we have left our first love, and that the graces of the Christian life are growing weaker within us! For how stands the case? We have just our own heart bearing conflicting testimonies: our heart tells us firmly that we are wrong now: it tells us, not nearly so firmly, that

we were right once : it may be erring on the favour-
able side, it *cannot* be erring upon the other : oh let
us judge of our own case as at the worst, since we are
yet in the place of hope : let us put the least favour-
able construction on our spiritual symptoms, when the
Physician of souls is yet offering to us the balm of
Gilead, which can heal and save ! What do you do
as regards worldly things ? Do you not always provide
against the worst that can happen ? If you must go a
journey, and are doubtful whether there will be rain or
fair weather, is it not wisest to go prepared for rain ?
If your little child has a cough, which may be only the
symptom of passing indisposition, but which may be
the premonition of that sad decline which will lay him
in his grave, is it not wise and prudent to apply to the
physician in time, and make sure of how the case may
be, while yet there is time to apply the remedy ? Let
us fix it then in our minds as a most solemn truth,
that the " fruit which shall remain," is that which
Christ especially desired and desires to see in His
disciples : that so the fruit which withers and moulders
is not that which He desires to see : that it is a most
alarming symptom of our soul's state when grace within
us seems to be declining and dying : that at the best
it means that we are losing ground which it may take
long time and labour to make up, and falling into sin
which will cost us bitter repentance ;—and that it *may*
mean that we never were in Christ at all,—that the
fruit in which we trusted was not the fruit of the Spirit,

—that we never have borne any of that fruit in which God is glorified, and in bearing which we are shewn to be the disciples of Christ. Yes, brethren, to any eye but His who can read what names are written, and discern what names are not written, in the Book of Life, the great test whether or not seeming Christian grace be genuine, is just whether it is permanent or not. It is not the warmest feelings, the most ecstatic raptures, the most abundant labours, yea martyrdom itself, for a brief season of excitement, that can prove that the work of grace is begun and is advancing in the soul. Never tell us, as infallible proof that a man has the mind of Christ in him, of his self-denying labours for a few months or years, of his long seasons of devotion, of his utter renunciation of the world its vanities and its wealth, of his longing desire to spend and be spent in preaching the glad tidings of salva-tion. Let us see him ten years after this,—let us see him thirty years after this,—and then see how all these feelings and purposes have worn! Let us see how they have stood the slow wear and wasting of long, common-place, matter-of-fact years! And oh, if the zeal have cooled and the fervour abated ;—if the minister who in his youth never grudged strength and life in his abundant labours for his Master above, have turned lifeless, careless, cold ;—if the visitor from house to house who was impelled to ceaseless exertion by love for perishing souls, has learned to smile at the Utopian fancies of departed days ;—if the worshipper who in youth loved the house of prayer, as a place where oftentimes his warmed, elevated, comforted heart testified to him that this was none other than the gate of heaven, is now ready at every call of business or of indolence to leave his place empty in the sanctuary, which now seems dull and cold: if all this be so, what shall we think,—what *must* the world think,—but that it was but the fervour of a quicker fancy and a faster pulse that was at the root of those seeming "fruits of the Spirit" which appeared in better days! But if it be otherwise,—and by God's mercy otherwise we know it oftentimes to be: if the path have been like the shining light, shining more and more unto the perfect day: then how hopeful and glorious a sight it is,—how cheering to the young disciple, looking forward with something of fear to the temptations and trials of the life before him. Oh, if the gray-haired minister, with less now indeed of phy-sical strength and mere physical warmth, yet preaches, with the added weight and solemnity of his long expe-rience, the same precious saving doctrines now, after forty years, that he preached in his early prime: if after these long years, he still sits by the dying man's bed, daily guiding him, with gentle assiduity, through the dark valley: if the philanthropist of half-a-century since is the philanthropist still, still kind, hopeful, and unwearied, though with the snows upon his head, and the hand that never told its fellow of what it did, now trembling as it does the deed of mercy: if the aged communicant, that never missed a sacrament for three-score years, still sits down gladly at the simple table, and confesses that Saviour who has fed him all his days, as solemnly and sincerely as ever: then, my brethren, I think even the world will believe that the religion of such men was a glorious reality. Years may indeed have calmed natural feeling down: the tear may not come so readily, and the heart may beat slower now: but the whole soul and spirit have grown into an unchangeable set through time: and the man could as soon cease to live, as to trust and love his Redeemer. Oh, far, far better, that ingrained, inevitable habit, than the fresher emotions of a younger heart! Such souls are indeed linked to the Saviour with hoops of steel,—or better yet, with those " cords of love," those " bands of a man," which no earthly power can sever. And surely, in the case of such, the Redeemer has " seen of the travail of his soul :" he has his disciples as he wished to have them: for is not this the very thing he meant, when he said to his apostles ere they parted,—" I have chosen you, and ordained you, that ye should go and bring forth fruit ;—and that *your fruit should remain !*"

Let us remark yet further, that not only is "fruit which remains,"—that is, a Christian profession which lasts on through life,—the only thing which can afford a man himself any well-grounded hope or assurance that he is indeed numbered among the saved and redeemed; it is also the only kind of Christian profession which will recommend religion to those who are not Christians. We all know quite well, that although it ought not to be so, men in general are very ready to judge of religion by the conduct and character of those who make a profession of religion. And just as a humble, consistent believer is a letter of recommendation of Christianity to all who know him,—letting his light shine before others in such fashion as leads them to glorify his Father in heaven,—just so is the inconsistent believer's life a stumbling-block in the path of his fellow-men,—a something to make them doubt whether religion be a real thing, and not a mere matter of profession and pretence. Every one whose duty has led him into such work, could tell you, that in practice and in fact, the inconsistent and unworthy conduct of professed members of the Christian Church, is what does more than anything else to encourage those who are regardless about religion to go on in their regardless way. Many a minister, when he points out to some conscientious man the duty of obeying the Saviour's farewell command, gets for answer, "There is such a one, there is such another one,—*they* are regular communicants: can charity itself suppose that they are true Christians." We do not say, brethren, that this way of thinking or speaking is right: for every man must bear his own burden, and other men's sins, or other men's neglect of commanded duty, will form on the day of judgment no excuse for ours.

But though this way of thinking be not sound, we all know that it is common: and oh my friends, how sorrowful a thought it should be to any Christian man, to think that, while perhaps he was giving of his means for the conversion of the heathen far away, he was by his daily life hindering the conversion of his next neighbour at home! And what so likely to do this, as to bring forth fruit which will not remain: to start in the Christian race all zeal, and alacrity, and eagerness; and then gradually to turn chill and apathetic? No one but God can tell how much harm is done by the minister who at his first entrance upon his work, sets agoing so many schemes as set the whole parish in a ferment, and then after some months or years of waning zeal, lets them all come to nothing: no one but God can tell how much harm is done by the private Christian, who in his new-born zeal disdains the quiet faith of old disciples who have long walked consistently, but whose zeal passes like the morning cloud and the early dew. Oh far better the modest fruits of the Spirit,—the "love, joy, peace, long-suffering, gentleness, goodness, faith, meekness, temperance," which make little show at first, but which *remain* year after year,—which yet warm the heart when flesh and heart begin to faint and fail,—which last while life lasts, and are made perfect in immortality! Nor let it be fancied, when we thus place permanence above mere zeal, and say that the "fruit which remains" is that which makes most plain to all men its divine origin,—let it not be fancied that we mean that a Christian profession which is warm and zealous cannot be lasting too,—or that to gain in permanence, the Christian character must lose something in zeal and warmth. Have we not known and heard of those, whose eagerness in the Saviour's cause might have been judged a mere fit of temporary enthusiasm,—something too eager to last,—if we had not found on inquiring that it had held on as warmly and energetically for twenty—for thirty years! And surely God is herein glorified,—surely Christian faith and practice are recommended to all men,—when the disciple thus "goes and brings forth fruit,"—and his fruit thus "remains."

And now, my friends, as we draw our meditation to a close, it is possible that some among you may be ready to say, that you are quite convinced how desirable and how necessary it is that the fruits of the Spirit in yourselves should be of this enduring nature; and that you wish no better than that, amid the wear of advancing years, amid all the changes in thought and feeling which these years bring with them, you may still feel your faith grow stronger, your hope clearer, your charity more kindly sympathetic: you may still keep the blessed views of your great Redeemer which first led you to His feet, and find Him in His house, in His Word, at His mercy-seat, as you have found him heretofore. Not for any new feelings and experiences do you wish, but only for the revival and the continuance of the old: and you long for nothing better on earth than for the quiet of Sabbath evenings long since past, and the happiness of old communion seasons.   You earnestly desire that yours should be the fruit which shall remain: but you fear that you are losing ground in these last days, and that it is not with you now as it has been heretofore: and you ask how shall the flagging resolution be braced into strength again, how shall the cold heart grow warm again, and the happy sense of God's favour be restored?   Oh brethren, the same power which implanted the better life within, must keep it alive day by day: the continual working of the Spirit must foster the fruits of the Spirit; and that Spirit is to be had for the asking in fervent, humble prayer.   Let us watch against the first symptoms of declension in religion: let us remember that spiritual decline begins in the closet: and let us pray earnestly and often, were it only to keep our souls in that habit of communion with God which is as a fence against all the assaults of Satan and of sin. Let us guard against that worldly spirit which is always ready to creep over us; and seek to walk by faith, and not by sight.   Let us be diligent in the use of all the appointed means of grace, and vigilant in guarding against every approach of temptation.   Let us seek to have our loins girt, and our lamps burning, as those who do not know how soon or suddenly the Bridegroom may come.   And so, through all the perplexing paths of life,—through all the cares before us, which may be many; and all the years before us, which may be few,—that best treasure within, of Christian grace, will go with us unimpaired and unchanged. Other things may go, so *that* "remains!"—remains in light and dark, in sorrow and joy, when the heart beats high with gladsome life, and when it flutters its last, and stops for ever. It will be a blessed support when we have little else to lean on, and a blessed hope when we can have no hope save that which casts its anchor within the vail. It will be our stay in death, and our passport to immortality. May God grant, then, that our Christian profession may hold out to the last; and that the "fruit of the Spirit" in our hearts, may be that "fruit which shall remain!"

X

THE DESIRE TO BE REMEMBERED.

"O Lord, Thou knowest: remember me, and visit me."—
JEREMIAH xv. 15.

LET us mark, my friends, the comprehensive request with which the prophet Jeremiah begins his prayer to Almighty God. "Remember me," he says: There are many things he desires, and he will in a little set them out in God's hearing: but the thing he asks first, as a fitting introduction to all the rest, and as indeed including within itself all the rest, is that God would not let him drop out of sight and thought. "O Lord, Thou knowest: remember me, and visit me." "Remember me!" That is his first and largest request.

We wonder how often these words are repeated in Great Britain, in the course of every day. We wonder how often, over the length and breadth of the world, during the same space of time, words which mean the same thing are repeated, in every form of human speech, and by all sorts and conditions of human beings. It might be curious if we could know this: but, without any positive information, we are certain of one thing, that there are very few shapes into which human thought can fashion itself, before it proceed from human lips, which it takes more frequently than this. Perhaps not even the perpetually recurring "God knows," which testifies how natural it is for us in our felt ignorance to turn to One who knows all, expresses a mood of thought more common to rational creatures. We doubt not that many, before the Deluge, bade those remember them, who should themselves be utterly forgot: we doubt not that when the parent of patriarchal days sent out his son to battle with the billows of life, he made and he received the simple request to be remembered: we doubt not that the dying mother, as she strained her eyes through the mists of death upon the features of her child, breathed low into his ear some words in her own forgotten tongue, in which, if we could translate them, we should recognise our familiar "Remember me," or some one of the other phrases which mean the same thing. And it is the same way still. It still falls cheeringly upon the heart of the dying, to think that some words and looks of theirs shall live in the remembrance of dear ones who are to remain behind them: and it still falls heavy on the exile's heart, if he thinks that amid scenes and among friends whom he remembers so well, his name, and his existence, are quite forgotten. So now, as ever, the parting friend says with a faltering voice, You will sometimes remember me when I am far away. So now, as ever, the dying whispers to such as were dearest, You will sometimes think of me after I am dead.

We have not spoken of those more ambitious minds, which have not been content that their memorial should be kept in the hearts of a few beloved friends; but whose labour it has been that their name, after they had passed from this world, should be remembered by multitudes. You know how entirely successful a certain man has been in carrying out his purpose; which was, he said, to leave something so written, as that men should not easily let it die. And you know how classic verse has bewailed the fate of those great and brave men who had no one to relate their doings; and whose doings and names have together gone into oblivion. For oblivion is the bugbear of ambitious men: and oblivion just means the condition of being quite forgot.

There is no doubt, my friends, that there are many things we wish, and many we shrink from, without much reason which it would be easy to set out. And this is certainly so with the common desire not to be entirely forgotten by those who once knew us and cared for us. And it is so, just as really with the desire to be kindly remembered · by the few near friends, as with that to be admiringly remembered by a crowd of strangers. The moralist has it all his own way in shewing the vanity of the desire, and the emptiness of the end. Say you are going away from your native land and the home of your youth: and you think, perhaps, that amid Australian wilds, or on the parched plains of India, it will cheer and almost gladden you to think that the dear circle far away is remembering you yet. Or when thoughts come over you of the days when you will no longer sit in your accustomed chair at home, and when they must learn there to do without you, you fancy it would almost soothe you on your narrow bed, if well-known steps came to your grave, and the tear of memory some-times fell on the grass which will grow over you. Well, says the moralist: what good will it do you to be remembered: what harm would it do you to be forgot!

We cannot answer him: but we do not mind for that. Enough for us that He who made us, made us so that by the make of our being we desire to be kindly remembered; and we shrink from the thought of being forgot. There is not one of us, who are accustomed to worship within these walls, that would like to think that if we never entered this church again, nobody would ever miss us.

Now, brethren, in words like those of the text, the prophet reminds us that this longing is in our nature: and he shews us the right direction in which to train it. In this short supplication, it is as if a kind hand took us; and pointing to the heaven above us, said, Seek to be remembered there! And there is a great deal taught us of the kindliness, condescension, and thoughtful care of the Almighty and Everlasting God, when we think of such a prayer as one that may without offence be offered to Him.   You feel that you are speaking to a real Person, in offering a prayer like this. Not to some vague, undefined " Great First Cause least understood,"—but to a merciful Father in Heaven; who looks down upon His child, and "like as a father pitieth his children, pitieth them that fear him."   It was while he looked on the kindly human face of Christ, that the whole heart's wish of the poor penitent thief went out in the "Lord, remember me!"   It was in special clearness of revelation of God's love to His poor creatures, that the Psalmist was emboldened to say, "I am poor and needy, yet the Lord thinketh upon me."   And it was addressing a Person, and not a "soul of the world," that the Psalmist expanded to greater fullness both the petitions in the text: saying, " Remember me, O Lord, with the favour that thou bearest unto Thy people; and visit me with Thy salvation!"

Let us dwell, for a little, upon the kindly and encouraging view of the Hearer of prayer, which is implied in the words of the prophet's petition.   When we call to mind that this petition was an acceptable one; that it was a petition which the prophet did quite right when he offered, and one that God approved; how much instruction, and how much encouragement, it gives us concerning God!

" Remember me," said the prophet, in his day of sorrow, to God. So you can see Jeremiah was not staggered, as he drew near his Maker in prayer, by that intruding doubt which will sometimes press itself upon the mind of all; and which we know did press itself upon the mind of even the inspired Psalmist. Did it ever come across you, my friends, as you knelt down in your closet to offer your evening prayer, Now can it be true that the Almighty God is indeed ready to listen to my poor words, and to consider my heart's desires: Can it be true that He, who has upon Him the care of all the universe, of all races, kingdoms, worlds;—in whose ear the praises of heaven are now resounding: Can such a God be really looking down upon me, this speck in immensity, this atom amid countless millions, this poor insignificant helpless sinful worm of the dust? David, Psalmist and King, knew the feeling. "When I consider thy heavens, the work of thy fingers, the moon and the stars which thou hast ordained; what is man, that thou art mindful of him? and the son of man, that thou visitest him?" Mark, my friends, here again we come across the two petitions of our text. The prophet might almost have had the psalm in his mind. David found it hard to think that God could remember man, or visit him: yet the prophet's prayer goes to just these two things: "*Remember* me, and *visit* me!" What a wonderful view of God is in that prayer! What a steady faith in God is in that prayer! *There* are the heavens, indeed; and *there* are the moon and stars: and *there* the little sinful creature of yesterday: yet he is sure that God can be mindful of him amid all the other things He has to mind : and coming, like a little child, to the great Father, the little voice pleads, "Do not forget *me !*" And it is not presumption ; it is faith, that speaks here ! Not a sparrow falls without our Father : not a hair on the believer's head but is reckoned : He compasseth our path and our lying down, and is acquainted with all our ways ! My friends, when you enter into your closet and shut the door, and pray to your Father which is in secret; be sure of *this*, that if your prayer be earnest and sincere, and offered in simple faith in Christ the Mediator and Intercessor,—you never spoke words to your nearest neighbour that he heard more distinctly, than the Almighty hears that prayer ! And He will not be impatient nor weary, though you ask His notice to your own little self, and your own little cares and concerns. You may tell to Him all those little things that really make up your life, though you would almost be ashamed to speak of them to a human being. You may make sure of a ready ear : sure of a kind sym-pathy : sure that you will not be condemned for egotism though you say ever so much about yourself, your own sins, and wants, and weakness, and toils, and cares. You may humbly go to God, and bespeak His attention to your own self ; saying, like the ancient prophet, without rebuke, "O Lord, Thou knowest : Remember *me*, and visit *me !*" And take for comfort, in your deep-felt insignificance, in your sinfulness and helplessness, the words of one of God's people, who felt all that you feel: " I am poor and needy: yet the Lord thinketh upon *me !*" Little child, amid your little troubles, very great to *you:* poor widow, scheming and striving to make the scanty shillings go their farthest, and plodding about your work with the heavy burden on your heart of how you are to make up your rent: oh believe it, that all these little things are known to the great God, and are cared about by Him; that He feels for you far more tenderly and thoroughly than any human being: that He knows all your little ways, and all your little cares: that you have not dropped out of His sight, or out of His mind: " I am poor and needy: yet the Lord thinketh upon *me !*" And you may press upon Him your small requests, and tell out to Him all that concerns you, saying, " O Lord, remember *me*, and visit *me !*"

I could willingly, my friends, say much more upon this matter: for I believe there are few things that add so heavily to the burden of many a Christian, and that take so much from that peace and rest which we might find in Christ, as a practical lack of faith in all this: a practical lack of belief that God knows all about us as He does: a practical belief that it is almost a profanation of prayer to tell God in it about a host of little things which really take up a great place in our heart and life. My Christian friends, let us in our prayers ask God for what we want: not for what we think we ought to want. Many a man, in

his prayers, speaks almost entirely about the things he
fancies it is the right thing to ask ; and says nothing
at all about a crowd of little wants and worries which
really are filling up his heart at the time ; and which
it would be an unspeakable relief to cast all the care
of upon God in prayer. Your heart is full of some
small anxiety or trouble : you are really thinking of
your own failing health and strength ; or of your little
sick child's pale face ; or of something amiss in your
business ; or of some slight mortification or disappointment, which has vexed you more than anybody
knows : yet you go to God's footstool and you come
away from it, without having said a syllable about
these things ; but having tried, with a wandering
attention, to pray for the conversion of the heathen,
or something else you did not then really and heartily
desire ; but which you thought a worthier subject for
prayer than yourself, and your own little selfish concerns. Now, brethren, you might perhaps get credit
from a human being for magnanimity and disinterested-
ness, if instead of asking from him something for
yourself you really wanted, you went and asked from
him something for somebody else you really did not
want. But just remember this : when you go to God
in prayer, you cannot mislead *Him* into thinking better
of you than the truth : whatever your words may be,
He sees the desire which is uppermost in your heart ;
and it is the desire, and not the verbal expression of
it, by which He goes. So that, in truth, when you

kneel in God's presence, you are in fact praying for the thing which God knows you are wishing for. He puts aside the words : He looks beneath them : He knows what it is you desire ; and why not openly tell Him, if your desire be a right one ? He knows you are thinking of your own little troubles, when you are praying for the Jews or the heathen. Oh, tell Him all about those troubles first ; and then you will be able heartily to add your intercessions for your fellow-men. But remember, for comfort, that God "thinketh upon" you : that He "knoweth your frame:" and that He will never blame you, though you go to Him with words like those of the Psalmist and prophet : "O Lord, Thou knowest : Remember *me*, and visit *me !*" You will think of that beautiful touch of nature, in a book by a great author. There, the father of a family, at a certain sacred and festal season, asks God's blessing upon him and his. All joined in the prayer · and after the others were silent, there came the little voice of a poor child that was a cripple, saying, "God bless us, *every one.*" Ah, *there* was the quiet outpouring of the little sad heart, eager not to be forgotten ! There was the "Bless *me*, even *me* also, O Father !" There was the sympathetic echo of the desire of the thirsting, weary, sinful heart of poor human nature, "Lord, remember *me*, and visit *me !*"

And in all *that*, there is no selfishness. It is not the wish to be distinguished and favoured above the other children of the family. It is but the wish to be even as the others ; poor, needy, sinful, as we know ourselves to be.   It is but that when Christ, the great Intercessor, speaks to Almighty God for Himself and His brethren of mankind, saying, in the name of all, " *Our* Father ; " the poor sinner should desire not to be left out : should put forth a trembling hand ; should lift up a feeble voice : should humbly urge his " *me, even me* also :" his " Lord, remember *me*, and visit *me !*"

And let us go on to remark another instructive and encouraging truth suggested by the prophet's prayer. "Remember me," said the prophet : and let us mark what simple trust in God's wisdom and kindness is implied in the offering of such a petition.   Everything is asked in that.   Jeremiah, indeed, goes on to add other petitions, in which we do not find it so easy to sympathise with him.   It is more pleasing to dwell upon such a prayer as that in which David does but set out more fully the request in our text, in words already quoted : asking that God would remember him for good, and visit him in mercy.   And better still, in its comprehensive meaning, and in its simple faith, is that prayer of the penitent thief, in which the single word conveys the whole desire of the poor dying sinner : " Lord, *Remember* me when Thou comest into Thy kingdom."   "Remember me :" *that* is the whole of the dying thief's prayer : and it is the best part of the psalmist's and the prophet's.   It was enough just to put one's self under God's eye : just to get God to think of one at all.   If God would but remember us, would but notice us at all; then it is taken for granted that He would see all that we want, and be willing to give it all.   Only to be brought under God's eye is enough : it makes sure of all.   My friends, what faith in God's wisdom and power and love, must be in his heart who really feels and believes *that :* who can offer that simple humble prayer, and then quietly and patiently wait at God's footstool, till in His own good way He answers it !   Say you wish to bring yourself under the kind notice of some kind and powerful human being : it is not enough to make sure that he should remember you : you must try and explain to him the circumstances that make you need his help so much : you must try and point out to him the ways in which it may be possible for him to help you. It is not so when you go to God, and ask His help. The broken-hearted sinner and sufferer that could never get through the miserable story of sin and sorrow that brought at last to the Saviour's feet, does not need to turn back those blotted leaves, and revive the miserable past, and moan over the hopeless future : Enough to lie lowly, in want and penitence, before Him who never cast out the penitent sinner ; and say, " Lord, remember me ! "   The thief on the cross did not need to tell the Saviour the history of his sinful life, or to point out to Christ the way in which to help him.   For all *that*, he trusted to One who knew his story since the day of his birth,—knew all his sins and all his temptations,—knew perfectly in what fashion to help and save.

And observe, too, that in such a prayer we take for granted not merely that God, without any formal telling, will know our case, and know how to help us: we take for granted that if He think of us at all, it will be kindly · that if He interpose at all, it will be in love. "Remember me," said the prophet, and said the penitent thief: there was no need formally to say, Remember me kindly,—Think upon me for good: *That* was taken as sure. You will remember how Joseph, in the dungeon, asked the chief butler to think of him; and said *how* he desired to be thought of. "Think of me when it shall be well with thee, and shew kindness unto me, and make mention of me unto Pharaoh, and bring me out of this house." And after all, we are told, "the chief butler did not remember Joseph, but forgat him." But in thinking of God, we feel that when David said, "Remember me, O Lord, with the favour that thou bearest unto thy people, and visit me with thy salvation," he really said nothing more than Jeremiah did, when he said, in fewer words, no more than "Lord, remember me, and visit me." No doubt, God sometimes remembers in wrath, and sometimes visits in judgment. When some sudden and heavy calamity befals us, it is not uncommonly called a divine visitation: in cases of sudden, inexplicable death, we sometimes hear it said, that such a one died "by the visitation of God." For there is an inveterate disposition in human beings to regard any uncommon event as *more* providential than one of everyday occurrence ; **and** to forget that every event is **exactly** equally providential ; and that everything that **happens in** this world, small and great, happens by the **visitation of God.** But though God does sometimes **visit in** wrath, *that* is not **the** way that most pleases **Him.** "**He doth** not afflict willingly, nor grieve **the children of men.**" And it was a merciful dealing **of God's** providence of which the Saviour spoke, when **He wept** over Jerusalem, and made mention of the ruin **that would** come upon it, because it knew not "the **time of its** visitation."

And observe further, **that** God's remembrance is an **energetic remembrance : it is not** a sentimental one. **He remembers us : He** sees our need : **and** then He **comes to help it.** There are people, who can look on **quite** contentedly at **the want** and distress of another **human** being, yet never **move** a finger to help : **there are** people who can even sentimentally mourn **over an evil which is** pressed upon their attention, yet **put** forth **no hand to mend it.** But oh brethren, if **we make our wants known to God in humble prayer** through **Christ : if we make known** to Him our sins, **our** toils, **our** temptations, our special needs in short ; then He **will** not merely "**think upon us,**" but "think upon us **for** good :" He will guide, comfort, enlighten, help, **and** save us. You will think of a striking proof, in **one of** the Epistles of the **beloved** Apostle John, how sufficient it is for our relief, that we should just tell the Almighty what our case is; how sure it is, that the want, remembered, will be relieved.   You know what is the greatest need of every human being: it is pardon and sanctification.   And St John assures us, that without any formal asking for these, it will suffice if we do but spread out in God's sight our need for them. "If we confess our sins, He is faithful and just to forgive us our sins, and to cleanse us from all unrighteousness."   Yes: only make known the want: bring it to God's remembrance: and it will be remembered practically; it will be relieved.   And you will think of the advice and the promise of the apostle Paul; and all it tells us of the blessedness that comes of laying down the burden of the weary heart at God's footstool,—of simply bringing it to His remembrance. "In everything," he says; "by prayer and supplication, with thanksgiving, let your wants be made known unto God."   And then, says the Apostle, if you do but *that*, hear the blessing that will follow.   "And the peace of God, which passeth all understanding, shall keep your hearts and minds through Christ Jesus!"

And so, my friends, you have seen how much comfort and encouragement we may draw from these few words of Jeremiah's prayer: you have seen how the spirit of them runs through the recorded prayers of all God's people: yes, and of those not God's people as yet, but who are but turning to God, and seeking after

Him. Doubtless, in their fullest meaning, this is the prayer of God's child, reconciled to Him through Christ; and drawing from experience the assurance of all the good that is implied in God's remembering us. Doubtless, there is a season in the history of the unconverted man, in which he can have no real desire that God should remember him: in which his real wish would be, to keep out of God's sight and God's remembrance. It is not the utterance of the natural heart, "Whom have I in heaven but Thee? And there is none on the earth that I desire beside Thee!" To stand alone, face to face with God: to be sure that every word and deed is going down in the book of God's remembrance: these are the very last things that the utterly worldly man would wish. Yet, brethren, while the words of the text may fitly set out the experience and the desire of those who have long been the Saviour's people, they may not less fitly serve as the expression of the first reaching after God of the awakened soul. "Remember me," said God's prophet: "Remember me," said the Psalmist, who had known God long: but "Remember me," too, was the prayer of the dying thief,—perhaps his very first prayer! And *that* prayer asks for everything! Pardon, peace, holiness: comfort and strength: guidance here, and glory hereafter! We who are here to-day have manifold wants: each has his burden, each his fears: yet we may all join with one heart in the "Lord, remember us, and visit us!" "Remember us" all: and "visit" us each according to his special cross and need!

We said, in beginning this discourse, that we wondered how many times a day, by human beings to human beings, those most familiar words that stand in the text are spoken: and in concluding the discourse, we may think how often those who thus simply seek to be remembered, are remembered as they desire. We would not set it down to want of heart, but rather to want of thought, when we call to mind how often the dead and the parted pass utterly from the memory: how completely and sadly true is that old adage which says that out of sight is out of mind. We can well believe, that in many a case where the promise never to forget, was given with the true purpose to keep it, time has slowly worn that purpose down: and now for many a day the grave once often visited is visited no more; and the far-away friend is all but quite forgot. I can think that it might be a pang to the heart of the Australian brother, if he could just look in upon the circle that gathers round the fire at home on a winter night, and see how very little they miss him. And perhaps the departed mother, that thinks of her child that she left behind her, even in the Rest above, might be saddened somewhat (if *that* could be) even *There,* if she could see her son going on his path through life, without one remembrance of her who watched over him in the days of infancy, and taught him his earliest prayers. No doubt, as we look at many human beings, it is interesting to think how much they may be remembering: but it is sad to think, too, how much they must have forgot. But if we make it our desire and prayer to be remembered by our Saviour and our God, we need not fear that we shall pass from *His* recollection! Amid all the care of this universe, He will stoop down to think of us;—of our little ways, and difficulties, and trials: we shall never be overlooked or forgotten by *Him!* In our weak faith, indeed, when days of darkness come, we may be ready to think that we have passed from His thoughts; and that He cannot be remembering what it is we are enduring. Ah brethren, there is no experience that we can pass through, which has not been anticipated by believers before us! Thousands of years since, *our* doubts and fears were felt; and God graciously took them away, with hopeful words which are ours as well. Listen to the ancient words of doubt; and to the blessed answer to them: Recognise your own doubts, and take the promise for your own.

"But Zion said, The Lord hath forsaken me, and my God hath forgotten me.

"Can a woman forget her sucking child, that she should not have compassion on the son of her womb? Yea they may forget, yet will I not forget thee!"

XI.

THE REDEEMER'S ERRAND TO THIS WORLD.

"For the Son of Man is come to seek and to save that which was lost."—St Luke xix. 10.

NOW, if such an incident as that described in the preceding verses of this chapter, had occurred somewhere close at hand within the last hour, we should have no difficulty in feeling, when we were told of it, that it had actually happened. We should at once see before us the whole circumstances: the Prophet of Nazareth in His garment without seam: the crowd of people that thronged Him as He walks along the street: the publican Zacchæus, little of stature, running on in advance and climbing up the tree: the kind Saviour stopping at its foot, calling Zacchæus down, saying a few kindly words that fairly bewilder the head while they go straight to the heart of the poor disreputable publican, quite unaccustomed to be spoken to kindly by people of any credit or character,—and then, amid the astonished murmurings of the crowd, going away to be guest at a house which it was long since any respectable man had entered. But it is far towards twenty centuries since all these things happened : and things look misty, and indistinct, and unreal, when we look at them over many hundreds of years. They seem like shadows, the people whose names and doings are preserved upon the historic page. They were not always names in a book : but now, in many cases, they are little 'more. Events recorded, are to events as they actually befell, what the embalmed mummy is to the living man. Let us try to bring back that day. Let us try to see these little things which took place upon it, as though they were going on now. The interest of these things ought to be, to-day, as fresh as ever. We see our Blessed Redeemer acting and speaking : mercy, sympathy, and salvation, in all He does and says.

He has stopped at the foot of the plane-tree, and called Zacchæus down. "To-day," says Jesus, "I must abide at thy house." Now Zacchæus was a publican. He was one of those Jews who were regarded as traitors to their country and their blood, because they had undertaken the odious work of collecting the tribute which the Romans levied upon the conquered race. And you know it is difficult for any man to continue better than the character he bears. The publicans, probably, were as bad as they were esteemed. And Zacchæus, probably, was no better than the average of his class. The Jews certainly spoke of him as "a man that was a sinner :" and we all know that although in theological phrase every man

is a sinner, yet when the word is used in the conversa-
tion of daily life, it always implies that a man is a
greater sinner than usual.   Zacchæus was the very last
man that the reputable Pharisee would have thought
of offering to go home with.   It was something new
to the poor publican, accustomed to averted eyes and
contemptuous glances, to find this great and good
Teacher treating him like a human being,—*also* a son
of Abraham like Himself;—to find this pure and holy
Prophet coming like a friend to his house, and sitting
at his table.   It was long since the poor publican had
been used to kindness and respect: there was something wonderfully fresh and new about them: and his
heart, so long shut up and hardened, welled out in
kindly charity at once.   That moment, he devoted
half of all his wealth to the poor; and declared that
he would restore fourfold all that he had ever unjustly
taken.   Ah, brethren, if Jesus had cast a stern look
up into the plane-tree, or if He had severely bidden
the publican to keep his distance, do you think *that*
would have converted Zacchæus and saved him?   No,
he would have gone home harder and bitterer in heart
than ever: and the next time he had tribute to collect,
he would have ground and squeezed and cheated worse
than ever.   But our Blessed Redeemer, notwithstanding this manifest and instant reformation which a kind
word had wrought upon the poor extortioner, knew
that some folk would find fault with what He Himself
was doing.   He is going towards the publican's house:

and He hears the murmur, perhaps only in self-righte-ous hearts, that says to Him, What are you doing there? Do you know into whose house you are going? You are going to an evil-doer's house ;—and not going as a judge, or as an officer of justice—*that* would be all quite right ;—but going as a guest, a friend. "He is gone," they murmured, "to be guest with a man that is a sinner !" As if He could have gone to be guest with any man who was not ! Am I here, the Saviour seems to say, in the house of a poor lost creature from whom you would hold apart ? Even you could not say worse of him than that he is quite a lost creature. Am I here ?—then I am just where I ought to be : "for the Son of Man is come to seek and to save that which was lost !"

How mercifully, you see, the Saviour puts the case ! How differently from the severe fashion in which the murmurers put it ! He is gone, said the murmuring Jews, to be guest with a man that is a sinner. He is gone, they said, to a bad man, a wicked man. They never think of his peculiar temptations : they never think of his secret repentance : they never think of that poor, weary, burdened heart, that needed but the slightest touch of kindness to make it melt and glow. They put the thing severely : gone to a man that is a sinner. The gentle words of Jesus seem to rebuke that severity. He does not say that He is come to save the cheating, griping, traitorous publican : No, He is "come to seek and to save that which was *lost."* No doubt, the Blessed One seems to say,—no doubt the publican *is* a sinner, if it comes to *that:* and so are you. But, He seems to say, we will not call him *that.* You will never win and save a man by calling him by harsh names. Let us take a word that shall speak rather of his misery than of his guilt. No, not sinner, though the word would be perfectly true. Call him a lost creature: call him a lost sheep: a poor, weary wanderer from the Fold.

And yet, merciful as it is, there is no undue laxity in Christ's estimate of sin. There is no shading away the evil of sin, and speaking of it as if it were no such very great matter after all. There is none of the cant which prevails in a certain portion of our literature, about human weakness, about strong natural propensities—about passion with its witching voice, which oft hath led men wrong. The essential evil that is in sin is not extenuated,—though of the two things which always go together in sin, misery and guilt, the Saviour puts prominently less the guilt than the wretchedness. No, there is no treating sin as a small matter here. You never can represent sin as anything much more serious than utter destruction,— final perdition and ruin and despair: and you see Christ describes the sinful soul as a thing lost,—He came "to seek and to save that which was *lost:*" and the very word which means the last and lowest extremity to which a human being can go down,—the word *perdition,*—as many of you know, it just means *loss:* it just means the state of being lost. And it is in that woful state that even the kind Redeemer puts it we are by nature: for the text was not spoken of Zacchæus only;—it describes the state and condition of every soul for whose sake Jesus came to this earth and died. "That which was *lost:*" that phrase names the condition of every soul with which the Redeemer has any concern. He came, He tells us expressly, "to seek and to save that which was lost:"—it is only with lost ones He has to do: if there be any mortal that is not lost, then *he* has no part in the Gospel salvation;—it was not for any save the lost that Jesus died. *Lost,* He says: oh surely *that* is not making light of sin. *Lost,* He does not say through whose fault; but the poor sinner would remember well. But while the Pharisee would say,—That man is a sinner, thank God I am not like him, let me stand off from him and have nothing to do with him;—Christ says, That man is lost,—he has wandered away like the lost sheep, and of himself he never would return,—the more need then that I should go to his house, and treat him like a human being: *that* may melt his heart and bring him back, —holding him at arms' length never will. Lost, and among such lies my occupation! I see my work, the Redeemer seems to say, wherever I see a lost soul. It was to seek and save such I came!

So, for one thing, we find in our text *Christ's*

estimate of *the condition of humanity.* It is something that is lost. Man is a *lost thing.* He is many things more. You may look at him in many lights. He is a toiling, hard-working creature. He is an anxious, care-worn creature. He is a weary, sorrowful, restless creature. But for the Redeemer's purpose, the characteristic that surmounted, and included, and leavened and ran through all the rest, was, that he is a *lost* creature.

Yes, brethren, we are *lost!* And what wide meaning, what unutterable sadness, are in the word, *lost!* What pictures are called up before our mind's eye by that word, that tells us what we are by nature!

We think of the poor wayfarer in the sandy desert, who has strayed from his path. He has lost all count of the landmarks,—he has hurried feverishly hither and thither, thinking he had caught some clue: his blood feels like liquid fire, his brain is in a bewildered whirl; and now, parched, fainting, despairing, he sinks down on the hot ground to die!— That man is *lost!*

We think of the gallant ship ploughing her way across the Atlantic,—a floating palace, a detached sample of all the science, and refinement, and might of the land, far upon the sea: we think of her, in the deceiving fog, steered at her full speed upon the huge ice-berg: then the sudden shock, the wild despair of most, the desperate efforts of some: the sudden partings, the wild horrible hurry and confusion, the water rising foot by foot, and then when the vessel made the last sickening plunge and went down, that final frightful cry of perishing hundreds, which was once described as having been heard on the shore eight miles off like a high faint prolonged wail, like the faintest murmur of an Æolian harp. They tell us that *that* sound curdled the blood of those who heard it. Yet all this horror we can crowd into the common-place statement, that *that* ship was *lost!*

Then we think again of some guileless youth, brought up in a pious home far in the quiet country, who must go out at length, like a bird from the nest, to stand on his own responsibility, and push his way in life far from a father's and a mother's care. We think of him, (ah! have we not known of him) falling from his early truth and integrity, beginning by petty pilferings, gaining gradually in hardihood, till some day the tidings reach the cottage far away that he, the clever boy at the parish school, the lad who was to make his parents independent in their old days,—that he has fled from justice to some distant country where he may join himself to desperadoes, himself as desperate ;—and the heartbroken father and mother never hold up their heads again. And all the neighbours who knew him, now look sorrowful when his name is mentioned: and every one who has a heart ever afterwards speaks the more respectfully and kindly to the poor silent old couple, whose darling boy is so sadly *lost!*

"So I lost her," wrote the kindly genius, as he told the story of his parting in childhood from the mother whom he saw no more. "It was in the fever we lost him, and then we lost heart," said the poor starving widow in her bare garret, when she told a humane visitor how her husband died, and she and her children sunk always lower in sorrow and want. "I have lost a day," said the Roman Emperor, when he remembered how on that day he had done no good. "That man is lost," we say of one who is placed in circumstances in which his powers, of body or of mind, are turned to no useful account. It would be easy to run up the induction of instances in which we use this word to convey a vivid meaning,—a meaning, for the most part, more or less sad. We have mentioned these that we may say, that in all these senses, and many similar ones, man is spiritually lost.

Yes, brethren, such is our natural state. No doubt our spiritual condition may be put in various ways. We are guilty creatures: we are depraved creatures: we are condemned creatures: in all these fashions, and more, you may truly and justly describe our spiritual state, and express those things about us which make us so greatly in need of a part in Christ's great salvation. But probably there is no single word which you could employ which gives so complete and comprehensive a description of man as he is by nature, as to say that he is *lost*. All error from the right way: all distance from our Heavenly

Father's house: all destitution, and danger, and impossibility of return, and imminence of final ruin; are conveyed in that one word, *lost!* Trace that word's meaning out into its various shades and ramifications: and you will find it implies, as no other can, all that we are; all that makes our need of the Saviour;—His sacrifice, His Spirit, His intercession. We are lost, as the wayfarer is lost, because we have gone away from our Father's house, and we are wandering in the wilderness;—in a wilderness where there is no supply for our soul's greatest needs, where we are surrounded with perils, and whence we can of ourselves find no way to return. We are lost, as the great ship is lost, for we have made shipwreck of our best interests; and we drive, without a helm, over the trackless sea of life; and, away from Jesus, we know no haven for which to steer. We are lost like the guilty child that by reckless sin has broken his father's heart; for, evil by nature, and worse by daily temptation and transgression, we are, left to ourselves, lost to holiness, to happiness, to heaven, to God. We have lost our birthright, lost our Father, lost our home, lost our way, lost our hope, our time, our souls! And what loss there is in our unimproved and unsanctified powers and faculties! How these souls are lost, in the sense that so little is made of what was meant for so much: lost as the untilled field is lost; as the flower which no man sees is lost; as the house built and then left empty is lost; as the

ship which rots in harbour is lost! Are not these
souls made for God's glory: ought not every power
about them to conduce to *that:* oh what loss of noble
possibilities unless they do! What glory ought we to
have rendered to God; what good to man: what
knowledge and happiness to ourselves! And if a
soul's whole powers and energies are given to the
mere supply of wants that end upon a present life
and world,—to the mere earning of the daily bread,—
is not that soul a noble thing *lost,*—a noble machinery
whose power is wasted and flung away!

In all these senses, and more, the Saviour's description of us is a sound and just one. Each of
us is lost. We have indeed the means of knowing
what was the Saviour's especial meaning when He
spake of us as such. It should seem from the para-
bles of the lost sheep and the lost piece of money,
that the thoughts present to His mind were, mainly,
that we are lost, in the sense in which any precious
possession is lost when we have no longer the use of
it; and that we are lost, in the sense that we have
wandered away and by ourselves never will return.
But in any case, the text reminds us of what the
Blessed Redeemer did for us in our lost estate. He
came to seek and save us.

Yes: "the Son of Man came to seek and to save
that which was lost." When we were lost, *that* was
what He did for us. Is it needful to repeat that old
story, that good news which never can be repeated

too often, but which I trust we all know and love so well, of how the Blessed Redeemer came to this world, and wore our manhood about his Godhead, and lived and died to save? Let us try to meet a difficulty which we may have heard not unfrequently stated; and which at the first glance appears to have much weight. Can it be believed, say some, when they read such words as those of the text;—can it be believed that Christ, the Creator and Preserver of countless worlds, would come to this little speck in immensity,—would live here in human form for three and thirty years,— and here would suffer and die, all "to seek and to save that which was lost,"—all to work out fallen man's salvation? And truly when in the starry night you look up at the glittering host above you, and think of their incalculable number and vastness, and remember how it is the creed of the philosopher, and, as some have maintained, the faith of the Christian, that each of these gigantic orbs, among which the earth is a sand-grain, has its own teeming population of rational and immortal life, do you not feel as the Psalmist felt, when he said in the contemplation of that grand sight, "What is man, that Thou art mindful of him, or the son of man that Thou visitest him!" Was it worth the Saviour's while to come down to so little a world, to seek and save a lost thing so very small!

Yes, brethren: reason and experience come in here to confirm the teachings of Revelation: it is quite credible, quite natural by the very make of all things, that the Son of Man, Creator of the universe as He was, should "come to seek and to save that which was lost." By the very make and nature of the universe, if a thing goes wrong, it becomes a matter of special interest. Suppose that some skilful engineer is watching the first trial of some great, complicated piece of machinery: suppose that a hundred pistons and cranks and levers go right, but that he sees away in a corner some little piece of machinery going wrong, jarring and straining: do you not think that the skilful mechanician will for the time forget all the rest of his engine, and concentrate his attention on that little thing that is wrong, till he has got it right? And even so we may think of the great Creator, as He looks upon the system of things playing beneath Him, turning away from a million worlds where there is no sin nor sorrow, where there is no jarring of the grand machinery, and coming down to this world that is wrong to set it right, to this race that is lost to seek and save!

Did not the man leave the ninety and nine sheep that were safe, and give his entire thought and energy to the finding of the one that had gone astray? That sheep had been an unnoticed unit in a mass: it was singled out, it became of importance, just by going wrong. A thing which never attracted attention when going right, often becomes a matter of much interest when it goes wrong. Some little detail in your household arrangements,—some little nerve in your physical frame,—you never thought of it,—but you are obliged to think of it now that it is jarring and tingling. And does not the sick member of the family awaken more interest, and get more care, than all the rest put together! How softly you speak to the dying ear: how kindly you clasp the dying hand: how anxiously you moisten the dying lips: how lightly fall the footsteps round the dying bed! You were kind enough, perhaps: but you know you never were so careful in the days of health and vigour. And have we not all been touched to see how the special care and fondness of the mother of a healthful, hopeful family, centre on her poor little deformed child,—that poor little thing that must face the toils and trials of life at so sad a disadvantage? And even so may Jesus look upon this defaced and deformed world;—the poor object amid a fair family of millions; the one, perhaps, in all He made that fell!—Or, to take a familiar instance, suppose a merchant is balancing his books at the end of the year: suppose that in his calculation thousands and thousands of figures are right, and only one is wrong: does he not fix upon the little error, and labour and labour on *that* till it is put right? And even so, we may say, does God hunt out the error that has crept into creation; does God efface the little speck which obtrudes itself upon His view. Yes, a thing becomes of consequence by going wrong. You know that if a man or a woman who never was heard of becomes suddenly a great criminal, then that crime-stained name is for a while in every mouth.   And even so, this world, so to speak, pushed itself into notice when it fell.   Ah, the little planet might have circled round the sun, happy and holy ; and never been singled out from among the bright millions of which it is the least.   But as it is, perhaps this fallen world's name may be on the lips of angels, and in the thoughts of races that never sinned.   *That* may be doubtful ; but we *know* that this world, by falling, gained a yet grander distinction than *that !* For three and thirty years it became the dwelling-place of the great Redeemer.   And we, when lost, as it might seem, in hopeless loss, were singled out thereby for the grandest, most precious, most glorious blessing, that, so far as we know, was ever given by the Almighty.   The Son of God left the glories of heaven to die for us.   The Son of Man came " to seek and to save that which was lost !"

It is indeed a mysterious thing, a thing not to be wholly explained by human wit, that the Son of God stood by till man had lost himself, and then came, at cost of painful quests, to seek and save him,—when we might think He could so easily have kept man from wandering at all.   Why let man fall, you would say,—and then do and suffer so much to save him ;—why not rather prevent than cure ?   The question, we grant at once, is one which we cannot entirely answer. We rest, indeed, in the firm belief, that great ends

must be served, and shall yet be seen to have been served, by man's permitted fall, by man's permitted **loss,** else sin and sorrow had never entered this creation. But there is one fact in the constitution of **our** minds which casts some little light upon this mysterious permission,—upon the fact that man was suffered **to** lose himself, before the Redeemer did so much to find him. **Is it not the fact,** that there is a peculiar satisfaction, **in** having **a** thing, great **or** small, which **was** wrong, **put right?** You have greater pleasure in **such a** thing, when **it** has been fairly set to rights, than **if it never** had been wrong. You have greater **pleasure in** finding **a thing which has been** lost, than if it never **had been** missing **at all.** Every one knows **this** who **has lived in the country, and** taken an interest **in the hundred** little **matters which** do **so** much there **to keep up** the interest **of life. Now we** know that our minds, **in** points **which involve no** sin, are made after **the** image **of** God. **So we are** justified, before getting any express **information, in** concluding **that our feeling is a faint re-**flection **of one** which may have place **in the mind** of **God: and** besides, **we** have express information upon **that matter;**—do **we** not **read, have we not** got it upon **the very** highest authority, **that "** there is joy in heaven **over one sinner that** repenteth, more than over ninety and nine just persons which need no repentance?" May we not think, that **apart** from those grand, inscrutable reasons which the Almighty has for permitting the entrance of evil into His universe,—those reasons which no man knows,—this fact of the peculiar interest and pleasure which are felt in an evil remedied, a spoiled thing mended, a lost thing found, a wrong thing righted, may cast some light upon the nature of the Divine feeling towards our world and our race? They are fallen, indeed, and evil; but they will be set right. They are lost, indeed; but they will be found. And when all evil that can be remedied is done away with, and when that evil which was remediless is turned by the Divine wisdom to conduce to the Divine glory,—may not this world seem better to its Almighty Maker's eye, may it not afford Him greater joy when He looks upon it,—than even when He beheld it, all very good, upon the evening of the Sixth Day? Ah, it was fair and beautiful then: it was right then: but it never had been tried: it had gone through nothing. Far more fair will it be to see, right once more, after being so sadly wrong:—sought and found, after having wandered away so far!

And now, my brethren, as we look once more at the Redeemer's gracious words, we think, Were there ever words so fitted to carry hope to the most despairing! What worse can you be than *lost!* Is not *that* just the word which the world applies to those who have strayed the farthest and sunk the lowest? You never can be worse than *lost!* All sin, all misery, are comprehended in that word. And yet, for you Jesus died. He did not undertake to save you in ignorance of the extremity of your case. He knew quite well how sick you were, when He undertook your cure: how far away, when He undertook to bring you back. You may have read that beautiful and touching story, which tells us how one who in the pride of intellect had reached within a few paces of the grave without ever betaking himself to Jesus was arrested at last, and brought to intense concern. But now he was filled with despair: and you may remember how this text came like a gleam of light upon his darkened spirit. "It is too late for me," he said: "too late, and I am lost." *Lost*, was the reply: then you are just the man whom Christ came to save: "for the Son of Man is come to seek and to save that which was *lost!*" And on his gravestone, besides his name and the number of his years, the same words stand to tell all his story. May they not tell the story of every soul in heaven? Lost, yet sought and found: Lost, yet sought and saved!

What more would *you* wish, my Christian friend, to be recorded of *you?* Do not these words tell where He found you, and whither He brought you, and what He made you, and what Blessed Friend it was that did it all? Lost by nature, lost by sinfulness, lost in misery, in depravity, in helplessness, in ruin, in despair! Lost utterly and hopelessly: yet sought, and found, and saved! God grant that each one here this day, may be able to take up for his own those beautiful words of a good divine and poet, whose beauty lies just in this, that they have so saturated themselves with the very spirit of the beautiful and hopeful text, of which God in His kindness has allowed us to think at this time!

Love found me in the wilderness, at cost
Of painful quests, when I myself had lost.

Love on its shoulders joyfully did lay,
Me, weary with the greatness of my way.

Love lit the lamp, and swept the house all round,
Till the lost money in the end was found.

'Twas Love whose quick and ever-watchful eye
The wanderer's first step homeward did espy.

From its own wardrobe Love gave word to bring
What things I needed,—shoes, and robe, and ring.

XII.

CONSEQUENCES.

"And Amaziah said to the man of God, But what shall we do for the hundred talents which I have given to the army of Israel? And the man of God answered, The Lord is able to give thee much more than this."—2 CHRONICLES xxv. 9.

HERE is a text full of practical wisdom and instruction. All of us may, by God's blessing, be the better for weighing and considering the things which are suggested to us by these words. But at the same time, there is nothing more certain than this : that *that* verse of Scripture might be understood in such a way, as that it should counsel to folly rather than wisdom : as that it should seem to point in a wrong direction, and not in a right one. For it seems to be a rule, running through all God's government of this world, that every good thing may be abused to a bad purpose : and God's holy Word itself like other things. You remember how St Paul said, speaking of even God's own law, that "the law is good, if a man use it lawfully." And in like manner, we may say assuredly, that God's Word will always lead us right, if we understand it rightly. But men have often understood it wrongly : and accordingly it has come to be, that some of the cruellest and wickedest deeds that ever have been done in this world, have been justified by the authority of the Bible. And more than this: when the Devil himself sought to tempt the Saviour to presumptuous sin, you remember that he did so with a verse of holy scripture. Let us pray, then, my friends, that the Blessed Spirit of light and truth may guide us to the right understanding of what the text teaches us.

As we go on through life, and gradually learn many things which we did not know nor believe in earlier days, there are few things which impress a thoughtful person more, than the difficulty of laying down broad general principles. We come to discern how much may be said on either side of any question. We come to discern that there are not many questions, bearing upon morality and life, that can be answered by a simple Yes or No. An unexperienced person states conclusions broadly, without any limitation or exception. He knows: he is quite sure: he has no doubt nor difficulty. Longer thought shews that there is something to be said on the other side. There is a curious instance, probably familiar to many of you, of the different ways in which men may think upon a very simple matter. You know the proverbial saying among us, universally accepted as a wise saying, that we should never put off till to-morrow what ought to be done to-day. And Procrastination, which just means a habit of putting off till to-morrow what ought to be done to-day, is universally esteemed as a wrong thing, and often as a ruinous thing. And no doubt, all this is sound and good. But still, there is something to be said on the other side. And accordingly, in Spain, which is a country especially rich in proverbial sayings, there is current a proverb which is just the direct contrary of ours. It is this: Never do to-day what you can put off till to-morrow. Now, our proverb is certainly the safer advice for most people; yet there is reason on the other side too. While our proverb cautions against procrastination, the Spanish proverb cautions against undue and inconsiderate haste. Its spirit, in short, is precisely the spirit of the saying current among us, that we should look before we leap. It means, in fact, that before doing anything, we should weigh the consequences of it:—we should think what it is to lead to. And, beyond all question, *that* is something which a wise man will try to do.

And so, we are brought back to the text; which suggests for our consideration precisely that subject. Almost any text may be made to speak what its writer did not mean: may be pushed into an extreme which is opposed to common sense; and to the teaching of God's Word taken as a whole. Especially is it so with this text. It might easily be treated in a rash and sweeping fashion, which would be very mischievous indeed. The advice it implies, must be cautiously and guardedly stated. This text is like a sharp edge-tool: very serviceable and quite safe in hands that know how to use it; extremely dangerous and mischievous in hands that do not. The subject brought before us in the text is the weighing of consequences. It is the looking before we leap. It is the propriety of considering what is to follow from what we do, before we do it.

Now here is a case in which there is much to be said on both sides. You may lay down sweeping principles on either side, which are at once true and untrue. They are true in a certain sense, and to a certain length. Beyond these, they are false. You may remember how a poet tells us of a certain great man, whose rule, through all his life, was Duty. Wherever placed, he inquired what it was he *ought to do;* and then he did *that*, or tried to do it. And the poet adds, by way of special praise of that great man, that he did it, "disdaining consequences!" He did his duty: he did right: and he did not care how people might like it, or what the result might be. Now, all *that*, in a certain sense, was very fine, and very noble. But, on the other hand, you could hardly ascribe to a man any greater folly than that he systematically shut his eyes to what might follow from anything he proposed to do. In a certain sense, it is the doing of a fool to disdain consequences : and it is the glory of a rational being that he can calculate, and weigh, and be guided by, consequences. It is just one great difference between an irrational brute, and a reasonable man, that the man weighs consequences and the brute does not. A drunkard, who for the sake of present gratification, disregards the ruin which he is bringing upon his children and himself, does most unquestionably disdain consequences. A young lad, who to supply some present want, steals his master's money, disregarding his own certainty of detection and destruction, and his parents' broken hearts, does certainly disdain consequences. A man who for the sake of worldly pleasure or profit, does a sinful deed, and thus draws down God's anger, and imperils and injures his immortal spirit,—disregarding Christ's question, "What shall it profit a man if he gain the whole world and lose his own soul?"—such a man does most assuredly and completely disdain consequences. And each of these three persons stamps himself a fool, just because he disdains consequences. To shut our eyes to the consequences of what we are doing, and blindly to rush on ; is madness. And yet, there are cases in which to resolutely refuse to take into view what may be the consequences of our conduct; is heroism : is Christianity in its highest and noblest development. When the three Jews in Babylon were told that the consequence of not falling down before the golden image would be, that they should be cast into a burning fiery furnace : When Moses saw, that if he cast in his lot with God's oppressed people, he must "forsake Egypt,"—must give up power and splendour and perhaps the throne itself : When St Paul was sure that if he turned preacher of the cross he must give up a peaceful life of comfort and esteem, and take instead a live of privation, toil, peril, contempt : in such cases as these, it was noble to disdain all consequences : it was noble to take the right path, in which God beckoned on ; and to leave the care of the results to God Himself !

I trust, my friends, we shall be able to clear up our thoughts on this subject, by considering the history which is brought before us in the text. I trust that it will make it plain to us, *when* we should weigh consequences and be guided by them ; and *when* we should disregard them, and refuse to take them into account at all.

King Amaziah came to the throne of Judah at the age of twenty-five : and, in the main, he did what was right in God's sight. Intending war with a neighbouring nation, he collected a great army of his own subjects. But he thought this army not sufficient ; and he hired, in addition to it, a hundred thousand soldiers from the King of Israel, paying for them a hundred talents of silver,—a very great sum. But when he was going forth to the war, an inspired prophet came to him, speaking in God's name, to tell him that these hired soldiers of Israel must not go with him ; and that if they went, God would make him fall before the enemy. Thus, you see, King Amaziah knew perfectly what was his duty. God had made *that* plain to him : his duty was to send away these soldiers of Israel, and to go to war without them. But the King was perplexed. He thought, What will be the consequences if I do all this ? There is that large sum of money, already paid away and gone. Perhaps he thought of other evil results beyond the loss of his money. Would not these Israelite soldiers, and their King, take bitter offence at the affront offered them, by dismissing them as not fit to go to war with the men of Judah? You can easily see what a crowd of difficulties and perplexities would rise up before poor King Amaziah's mind, when he considered what would come of his obeying God's command in the matter. For people then, doubtless, were ready to take offence when slighted, just as now: and a hundred talents was a large sum to throw into the sea, and to make up one's mind was to go away and bring no return. But the King mentioned to the prophet just one of his difficulties: the more tangible and apparent one. "God bids me send away those Israelites," Amaziah seems to say: "and of course what God commands, is my duty. But then see the consequences. What shall we do for the hundred talents which I have given to the army of Israel?"

There was the King's difficulty. The prophet's answer to it we shall think of in a little while.

Now, brethren, I do not say that Amaziah did wrong in naming that loss of money to the prophet. He could not help its occurring to his mind: no reasonable man could have helped it: and it is a great comfort, in any perplexity, not to keep it like a cold dead weight on our own heart; but to talk it out frankly to one who can feel for us and feel with us.

But Amaziah was wrong in this: that he seems to have regarded this difficulty as a fatal objection to his obeying God's command. Instead of saying, "Well, God's way must be right; and though I must lose that money, which is a great thing to me, if I obey God's direction, yet my course is clear: I must obey God, and accept the consequences: I must obey God, and let the hundred talents go:" instead of saying *that*, Amaziah seems to say, "Well, that is God's command, no doubt; but I really cannot obey it; for I cannot make up my mind to lose those hundred talents I have already paid for the help which He bids me forego." Amaziah, in short, not merely states his difficulty; but he seems disposed to act upon his difficulty. And *there* he was wrong.

And this brings us to the great principle which should guide all wise Christian people in regard to the consideration of consequences. The rule is this: there may be great difficulty in applying it in individual cases, but there can be no doubt as to the soundness of the general principle: Wherever we are sure that duty leads: wherever we are sure God bids us go: then *that* way we should go, whatever and however painful the consequences may be. In all other cases, a prudent Christian man will carefully weigh the consequences of what he may think of doing, and be guided by the consideration of them. But if God clearly points the way, *that* way we ought to take, disregarding consequences. Martyrs have found that the consequences of going where God commands, were painful and repulsive to human nature: there have been Christians who found that God's way led them to the stake and the scaffold, and the bloody arena with its savage beasts. Yet *that was* the way. It was plain and clear. There could be no question that the right thing was to confess Christ before men, whatever might come of it: there was no forgetting the Redeemer's own words, that whoever should deny Him before men, He would deny on the Judgment day. The way was plain: and as for the consequences, they must just be taken. There was no help. Only by denying the Saviour could these consequences be escaped: and the thought of denying Him could not be for one moment admitted. I doubt not, brethren, that many a faithful witness for the Cross and the Redeemer, had his thoughts like those of the King of Judah. I doubt not many martyrs have said to themselves, But what shall we do for the wild beasts, and the fiery stake! I doubt not, their eyes were quite open to the result of their holding fast their profession. But yet you know what numbers of men and women are reckoned in the noble army of the martyrs: you know how, by God's grace and strength, many a weak human being was enabled to " disdain consequences," in a higher and nobler sense than *that* ever was done by the most resolute man in his own unaided strength. For the rule was clear. We must hold right on, where God leads us; looking for God's promise to be fulfilled, that as the day, so shall the strength be. In short, my friends, the rule is, that we are to do right; and as for the consequences, leave them with God. No unworthy shifts: no paltry diplomacy: no fear of men, nor crafty arts to manage them: Let us do right, and trust in God!

And remember, brethren, we are to do all that, humbly. We are not to do it in a boasting, vain-glorious spirit. We are not to do it in any strength of our own: but in simple reliance on the promised grace of God. It is not the man who is most confident beforehand, that is most to be relied on when the day of trial comes. Not the man who says, with Peter, I never will deny Thee: but the humble man who stands in doubt of himself, and who bends lowly at God's footstool, saying, Grant I never may! We have all heard people talk in a vapouring manner about their determination that nothing should turn them from the path of duty. I have heard a man say that if the road were lined with cannon, he would do a certain foolish thing, which he had hastily and foolishly said he would do: and which, at the time, I daresay he was very sorry for having said he would do. For often-times people try to bolster up a failing courage with big words. And the people who talk in that boastful way, are very frequently not people who are doing right, disdaining consequences; but who are doing wrong, disdaining consequences. My brethren, the grand thing is, not that a man should say that he will go on in the path of duty, whatever loss *that* may bring him: but that those around him should see that he *is* going on in the path of duty, though that should not be the path of worldly gain. And we know, that in the old days of martyrdom, when men's constancy was tried by tests by which *we* may be thankful that our weak faith is *not* tried, it was not the men who spoke most confidently beforehand that quitted themselves most manfully when the day of trial came. Men who had boasted of the courage they would shew: men who had pushed themselves unbidden in the way of martyrdom; have proved recreant at the last; and, like the over-confident apostle, have denied their Lord, in the presence of those tortures of which they had spoken lightly in former days: while humble souls, that felt and confessed their own utter weakness, have borne nobly the trial to which they never had trained themselves to look forward but with many fears: have found that God's strength is made perfect in the weakness of his own: have felt the martyr's strength come with the day of martyrdom: and you know God never promised it would come till the day that needed it. The true proof, brethren, that a man disdains consequences, is that he should disdain them; not when they are in the distance, *coming:* but when they are present realities; when they are *come!*

Now, my friends, this subject is a most practical one. It will concern every one of us, at many points in our pilgrimage path. The same difficulty which Amaziah felt, many among us will be made to feel from day to day. The time will often come, in which we see plainly enough what is the path of duty; but are tempted to ask, What shall we do for the hundred talents? Ay, and for much less than a hundred talents. There is many a professing Christian who is very un willing to miss a little advantage, a little money, or to get a little ill-will, by doing what is right. *There* is the way that God bids us go. Whenever there are two paths before us, one wrong, and the other right, we may be just as sure that God means us to take the right one, as if He told us so in an audible voice. But then, what shall we do for the hundred talents? What shall we do for that gain and advancement which honesty would lose, and which a little judicious trim- ming could get? What shall we do for the obloquy and the enmity which the straightforward course will bring, and which a little yielding would escape? There can be no doubt at all, my friends, that in this world, honesty is often the very worst policy. There can be no doubt, that a certain flexibility and elasticity of soul and conscience may make a man get on, as con- cerns this world, when rigid integrity would stand in his way. Nothing would be easier than to mention striking instances, in which men threw away their chance of the highest places by an act of injudicious honesty; and in which a little toadyism, a little sneaki- ness, a little sinking of the downright honest man, paved the way to the greatest worldly advancement. And the same law holds in lesser things. A trader who never puffs his wares as better than they really are; may not drive such a business as the brazen individual who never spares the trumpet. A preacher who sets forth sound doctrine to people who have not been accustomed to it, and who do not want it; may make himself, for a time, obnoxious enough. There are people who will think you their enemy because you tell them the truth, and their friend if you flatter them with smooth words of falsehood. But, brethren, let us do right still! Let us speak the truth, and live the truth, no matter what we may lose by it! Worldly success may, perhaps, be gained by unworthy means: but we will not have it at the price! Let us do God's will, my friends: let us go where God bids us go: disdaining consequences! Our business is to do what He commands us: and we leave it to Himself, to say what shall be the result!

And, as help and encouragement to do all that, let us go on a little farther with the subject. Let us look to what was the prophet's reply to the difficulty started by the king. Amaziah said, "But what shall I do for the hundred talents which I have given to the army of Israel?" And the prophet answered, "The Lord is able to give thee much more than this." Lay *that* to heart, my brethren! In the long-run, no man will ever lose by obeying God's bidding. And just as assuredly, no man will ever gain by disobeying it

Yet, remark, poor king Amaziah was quite right in his fears as to what might be the consequence of sending away the army of Israel. It cost him a struggle, we may well believe: but he did obey God's command. He saw the consequences: but he trusted God, and took his chance of them. And sure enough, the consequences followed. He lost his hundred talents: and more than that, the Israelite soldiers, angry at their dismissal, wrought mischief to Judah on their way home. They were mortified, no doubt: they were deprived of their opportunity of plunder, and of renown among their own people: "They returned home," we read, "in great anger;" and on the way, they revenged themselves, by falling upon the cities of Judah, and smiting and spoiling them. All these evil consequences came: and came just because Amaziah obeyed God's word. Yet remember the prophet's declaration. Besides the simple obligation to obey God's will, the prophet tells the king that it was well worth his while to obey it: that though he might at the first lose by obeying God's will, he would gain far more than he would lose. Yes: to go where God commands, and to do what God commands, though loss may come of it, is truly not a disdaining of consequences: it is a fuller and truer weighing of consequences! It is to look farther on: it is to throw Eternity into the scale of duty and interest: it is to draw the wise and sound conclusion, that what is wrong, can never be truly expedient; because it would be no profit, none whatsoever, to gain the whole world, and to lose the immortal soul! There are always consequences from our conduct, whether we go this way or *that:* and the wise man will weigh the consequences upon either side. And the prophet asks the king to do just *that:* telling him that if he does it, he will see that the true gain is all on the side of obeying God. On the one side, there were a hundred talents: on the other side there was the favour of God: and the question for the king to consider was just this; which was worth most? And many a time, in little things and great, we are all brought to just that choice, and that calculation. The immediate consequence of our doing right, may be that we shall make a loss: and we may feel it hard to resign our minds to the loss of the hundred talents,—the little gain in money, in standing, in pleasure, in advantage of any kind, that we might easily get by doing wrong. But oh, let us always look, for the confirmation of principle, and of the determination to take the right way, to the farther and greater and longer-lasting consequences:— God's blessing on the honest and right way, God's wrath and curse upon the wrong and false way! And never forget, that if in this world the consequences of taking the right way be sometimes loss, and misconception, and undeserved reproach, and failure and coldness of friends: if the man of high principle and scrupulous honour may oftentimes fail to reach the worldly place and profit which men of lower tone and more elastic conscience succeed in grasping: if pliable and squeezable men are found to rise high both in earthly gains and earthly reputation: never forget that the next world will set all *that* right: the next world will redress the consequences of all human doings. And never fail to set in the front of all your calculations of the consequences of what men do, the Saviour's memorable question, "What shall it profit a man, if he gain the whole world, and lose his own soul!" Yes, upon the most prudent counting up of loss and gain, it was worth while to be a martyr! And if the scorching stake, or the bloody scaffold, could be escaped only by denying the Redeemer; then deliverance from these things was too dear at the price!

So I do not ask you, my friends, in asking you to make up your mind that, by God's help and grace, you will make God's will your rule, and walk where God points your way; I do not ask you to disdain consequences: I ask you to weigh the consequences of all your conduct, carefully and deliberately. Only see to it, that you remember that there are consequences of all we do, which reach on through eternity: that our "works will follow" us beyond the grave, both in the character they stamp upon us, and in the awful responsibility which comes of this truth, that we must answer for every word and deed at the throne of judgment. It is indeed a miserable and unworthy thing, to weigh consequences in that petty fashion in which many do: and, when duty is plain, to be always thinking, What will such a one say? Won't this give offence to such another? May not all this do me harm, somehow? My friends, if God has made the path of duty plain before us, then let us sweep all *that* away! If God tells us that we must give up the hundred talents, then in God's name let them go! Let them go, though no recompense should ever come, just because God bids us! Let them go, gratefully remembering that God can give us much more than this: that there never was a sacrifice made by man for God's sake and at God's bidding, but God has requited, and will requite, a hundredfold. Take no man's word for *that:* listen to the words of the Redeemer! "And every one that hath forsaken houses, or brethren, or sisters, or father, or mother, or wife, or children, or lands, for My sake, shall receive an hundredfold, and shall inherit everlasting life." Let us go where God bids us, brethren, though the way be rough and steep: it is enough that it is *His* way. Let us trust God, and do right: and it will all be well in the end!

XIII.

NO MORE PAIN.

" Neither shall there be any more pain."—REV. xxi. 4.

THERE is no need to explain to any human being what it is that is meant by Pain. We all know *that*. We know pain by the best means of knowing : we know it by having felt it. And we arrived at that sad knowledge early : none of us lived long in this world, before learning by experience what is meant by pain.

There is a sense in which we may use the word, in which its meaning is wider than it is as it stands in this text. *Pain* may be taken to mean all suffering, whether of the body or of the mind. And when we speak of Pleasure and Pain ; or of things being pleasing or painful ; we sometimes understand by pleasure everything that is pleasing, joyful, happy : and by pain everything that you would shrink from, from whatever source it may come,—everything that implies suffering, sorrow, anguish. But it is not in this large sense that the word is to be understood in this text : Pain is here to be understood in its strict meaning. For you observe that the writer of the Revelation distinguishes it from sorrow, from death, from tears: and as he tells us of the glory and the bliss of the New Jerusalem above, as he tells us of the springs of anguish that shall be absent there, he classes our sad heritage of suffering by itself. He is speaking of God's own people, when from the discipline and trials of this mortal life, they shall have passed into the Golden City: and he tells us that in that life immortal, "God shall wipe away all tears from their eyes: and there shall be no more death, neither sorrow, nor crying; neither shall there be any more pain."

So it is manifest that in this promise, pain is to be distinguished from that which is properly called sorrow: and we are to understand by pain that which the word strictly means: to wit, suffering which arises from our fleshly nature. All feeling, of course, pleasing or painful, is in the soul: it is the soul alone that *feels.* But pain means bodily suffering. Pain means *that* suffering which though felt in the soul, has its origin in the body. *That* is pain. And now you see that in the better world, there is to be an end of it. "There shall be no more pain."

I feel, my friends, that it is almost impossible for me to present to you this blessed promise in such a fashion as may make you understand its real force. For who needs to be told, that it is only when a man is actually pressed by pain, that he knows what an unspeakable blessing it is to be free from pain: and who does not know how poorly and ineffectually any words that human lips can utter, labour to convey to another the terrible, crushing, overwhelming Fact, that is meant by words so easily said as *Great Pain?* Ah, words are idle to express the thing as it is: only the great sufferer knows what is meant by great suffering: only he knows the value of release from suffering: and even he forgets it when the suffering has passed away. And how then, my friends, shall I make *you* feel, sitting there quietly and comfortably this Sunday afternoon, what is meant by the promise of "no more pain!" There may be those among you now, who feel some little twinge or ache: and even such will more feelingly understand the force of the text. But in by far the most of you, there is now, I doubt not, perfect freedom from pain: heart, and head, and limb, are right: the entire bodily machinery plays without a jar. How shall we understand and realise the value of that absence of pain which has grown to us a thing so common and so cheap! Let us try to recall the days of suffering we have known! Let us call back the days when we learned that the spasm of some little nerve, that a little inflammation of muscular tissue, that a little extra pressure upon brain or heart, might bring long nights of sleepless agony,—might not merely destroy utterly the enjoyment of life, but unfit utterly for the duties of life: let us think of the anguished face, and the convulsed limb, and the deadly chill and faintness, that have come with pain : let us think of the sudden insight which in such moments we have had, into the tremendous depths of misery which these poor natures of ours can bear without annihilation : and with such remembrances in our hearts, let us, praying for the direction of God's Holy Spirit, address ourselves to the consideration of the solemn lessons as well as the blessed encouragements, which this text may fitly suggest to us.

In the better world above, then, pain shall be unknown. And although, my friends, I am more and more persuaded by longer experience, that it is the deep sense of God's love and mercy in Christ to us poor sinners, and a responsive love and gratitude and trust in our Blessed Redeemer and in God manifested in Him, that shall draw our souls to God, and lead us onward in the path of life, far more than any mere dread of Hell as a place of insufferable pain, or any mere wish for Heaven as a place of unspeakable glory and happiness ;—still, brethren, different motives work with especial power upon different human beings; and the wish to escape woe and to attain happiness is placed in the nature of all of us by our Maker, and is not intended to be ever eradicated : and it is very fit and right that our longings after the Paradise above should be quickened by thoughts of its blessedness ;— of all the happiness which shall there be present : of all the anguish which shall thence be far away. Many a poor sufferer, doubtless, will cherish a very soothing and cheering thought of Heaven, as the place,—as the only place in all the universe,—where there is "no more pain." And even those who have never experienced very prolonged, or very overwhelming suffering, will hail the like assurance with great delight. Pain is, in itself, never a desirable thing. Great good may come through it, or of it : and we may be content to bear it for the good that is to come of it : but the actual suffering, in itself, must always be a thing from which we would, if it were possible, shrink away. No man can like to be in pain, for the sake of the pain itself. You know how pain, even when not very great, and even when not likely to be followed by serious consequences, destroys the enjoyment of life. A thousand blessings may be neutralised, so far as concerns their power of making us happy, by one little fretting pain. Say it is a beautiful evening of summer, and you are looking at a sweet country landscape : you know that acute suffering, present in the little nerve of one tooth, will effectually call off your attention from all the beauty that surrounds you,—will utterly destroy your enjoyment of it all. You know that if a man were surrounded by all conceivable worldly advantages : if he had a charming home, and abundant wealth, and all the comforts and elegancies that abundant wealth can buy : still if he were in ceaseless pain,—if day and night he never knew release from the gnawing, wearing, depressing grasp of bodily suffering, he would lead but a dreary life after all. For pain is a thing that you cannot well forget while you are enduring it : it has a wonderful power of compelling attention to itself : you cannot long or heartily think of anything else, while you are suffering acute pain. How long it makes the hours seem : how weary the night : how blank the day ! But pain does worse than mar the enjoyment of life : it unfits, as a general rule, for the work and duty of life. No doubt, there have been men who did nobly the work God set them in this world, even with all the disadvantage of being burdened with almost ceaseless pain : no doubt, there have been men who, even with all that disadvantage, have been able to form sound and hopeful views of human affairs, and to sympathise heartily with the cheerful no less than with the sorrowful : possibly some of us may have enjoyed the privilege of knowing those who, even with all that disadvantage, have produced such beautiful, touching, and far-reaching thoughts, as have moved the heart and formed the mind of thousands. But this is not the common way in which things go. As the general rule, you cannot do your work well when you are suffering pain, even if not very great. It worries you : it draws off your attention from what you are about : you have no heart for your task : you cannot put yourself at it in that thorough, earnest, energetic fashion in which you must go at any work which you would wish to do well,—which you would wish to do to the very best of **your ability.**   And there are worse possibilities about pain than **even these.**   I do not forget that by **God's** Blessed **Spirit's** working, **it has** often been sanctified **to work the soul great good :** it has served to wean **the affections from the things of** time and sense : **it has been like the furnace-fire in** which **the soul has been purified** like **some precious** metal.   But **this, brethren, is the tendency of pain** sanctified : **it is not the simple and natural tendency** of pain.   **Do not you know that pain just as frequently** makes **the sufferer fretful and impatient : peevish and** ill-tempered **to those around : nay, ready to repine at** the allotment and **providence of God !**   **"Curse God** and die" **is just as natural a tendency of pain, as is** **"Father, let this cup pass** away ; yet **not My will, but** Thine, **be done !"**   **And if we have heard of those** whom sanctified suffering purified **and elevated and** refined, **till through the worn features you could** almost **see the angel's nature ; who is there but has** heard of, **and perhaps has seen, instances in which** protracted **suffering, acting upon an unrenewed heart,** has developed **a wrath, a bitterness, a defiance of God,** a malignity towards **man, that looked like the demon** incarnate !

And thinking **of all these things about pain : think-** ing of the unutterable anguish **it sometimes means :** thinking of how it may embitter **life and unfit for duty,** and **bring to** a spiritual frame **the most hardened** and fearful ; — well may **we hail** with **delight the** assurance, that there is a world where it shall be unknown. No pain in heaven! No little irritating disquiet: no sharp piercing pang: no great overwhelming agony, that tells its tale in groans and shrieks, that wears out life, that racks and maddens! Yet not that it shall be *there*, that you escape pain by giving up pleasure: not that you cease to feel pain, because you cease to feel at all. No: the soul in glory shall still be invested with a bodily frame the most delicately sensitive: alive to every thrill of bliss: feeling all feeling with a keenness and intensity never known before: the perfection, in short, of a sensitive material nature: a nature which, doubtless, *could* feel suffering with fearful reality, if suffering could ever come there. But in that better country, there shall be absent for ever, the cause in suffering, no less than the signs in tears: for "there shall be no more death, neither sorrow, nor crying; neither shall there be any more pain !"

But all this naturally leads us to ask, If pain be so bad a thing, and if it be so happy an assurance that the day is coming when there shall be no more of it, why is it here at all? Why is there such a thing now? Well, brethren, I do not think it would stagger our trust in God's wisdom and goodness, even if we could find no answer at all to that question. It would only be part of the great question as to why Evil is at all permitted in this creation: and the answer to that question is one of those secret things which belong to

God. But in the matter of pain, we can, in so far, answer the question. We can discern several important uses which are served by pain : and we can discern, too, that pain will not be needed for these uses in the better world. It will not cease, till its occupation is gone. The lessons it is meant to teach us, will not be wanted there. They will be well remembered, without our having pain ever (so to speak) at our elbow to remind us of them.

For what are the lessons which are taught us by pain ?

Pain teaches us, for one thing, how feeble and dependent we are. If any man were foolish enough to think that he might set up for himself, that he might go on for himself, that he could do without leaning at every step and every moment upon the arm of God,— I think pain would convince him of his folly. What a humbling thing great pain is ! How it takes down pride and obstinacy : how little power it leaves us to think of the impression we may be making on others ! The proverb says that pride feels no pain : only let the pain be great enough, and where will be the pride ! I call to remembrance a certain scene. It is in the beautiful city of Cæsarea. It is the theatre : a vast crowd is assembled : there is a magnificent throne : and on it sits a king. His robe was of silver tissue, and shone brilliantly in the morning sun, as he made an oration, no doubt in arrogant enough terms, to certain people who had offended him. So august was his appearance, so lofty his language, that "the people

gave a shout, saying, It is the voice of a God, and not
of a man!" Herod half believed them! You can
imagine that, if not a God, he looked every inch a
king. But in that moment, a fearful, overwhelming
agony grasped him: and the poor miserable wretch,
still in his grand dress, was carried out, groaning and
shrieking, and smitten with a horrible loathsome death.
Oh what a mockery of his grandeur, a minute since!
Oh what a scoffer at human pride, what a teacher of
human dependence and helplessness, is overmastering
pain!

And for a second thing, pain is something to remind
us of the Evil of Sin. Not but what sin's badness
dwells in itself, apart quite from any sad consequences
that flow from it: but there are many souls, somewhat
blunted and dull in perception, who can discern more
vividly that physical agony is a bad thing, than that
moral evil is a bad thing. And just as the index on
the dial of the barometer, as it goes down and down,
is something to tell of the impending hurricane; so all
the pain that darkens this world is something to indi-
cate how bitterly bad a thing is sin. Every child
knows, that had there been no sin, there would have
been no pain: and the worse pain is, the worse it
proves sin to be. And so pain is an ever-present
reminder of a thing we are all far too ready to forget.
Oh, if we could interpret pain aright,—if we could
remember its meaning every time it shews us its sorrowful features,—how constantly we should have im-

pressed upon us how fearful a thing is sin ! You have
every one of you known pain : Well, just fix this in
your minds, that all the pain you have ever suffered,
was the effect of sin. You never would have had a
headache, if it had not been for sin. You never would
have known a sleepless night, a shooting pang through
the nerves, or a dull weight at the heart, if it had not
been for sin. If it had not been for sin, this world
would never have seen faces sharp with pain ; nor
forms wasted with pain. There would have been no
hospitals nor infirmaries : no need for science seeking
agents that might dull to suffering by dulling to all
sense : none of that sad literature, so interesting yet so
sad, that sets out the nature and causes and remedies
of the countless pangs that flesh is heir to. Now,
brethren, we need to have it pressed home upon us,
and pressed often upon us, that sin is a bad thing.
Our natural tendency is to think to ourselves, Oh, sin
is not right,—it cannot be justified,—it *is* bad no
doubt,—but it is not such a very great matter after all.
—What does pain say to *that*, think you ! You know
whether pain, crushing, intolerable maddening pain,
is a small matter : and pain, remember, is only one
sad consequence of sin : pain is sin manifesting its
tendencies in only one direction : there are a score of
evil things and tendencies about sin besides this ! All
the agonies you have ever felt, ever seen : all the anguish which even stout-hearted men have said would
have driven them mad, if it had lasted but a few

minutes longer: all that has ever left its trace on the ghastly face and the hollow wistful eye: all *that* has been something to tell us that bad as *it* may be, there is something worse,—something of whose intense unmingled bitterness it is but a faint, feeble manifestation,—and *that* something, *that* black, mysterious, awful something,—sin!

And another lesson taught us by pain, is suggested by this: **It is how terribly** God can punish:—what tremendous appliances of punishment He has at His **command. I** have no taste for dwelling **on** such a **subject: I** would rather think of the love of Christ **than** of terrors of judgment: but we must face the **truth,** my friends. You cannot do away a fearful fact, merely **by** turning **your** back **upon it.** A thing does **not cease** to be, **because you** may shut your eyes and **refuse to see it.**—Now, my friends, people sometimes **say, God is** merciful,—**He is all** love,—He will never inflict upon His poor creatures such terrible sufferings **as** seem to be threatened in certain texts of the **Bible. Brethren,** what does pain, **the** pain we have ourselves **felt and** seen,—what does *it* say to such a thought? **What fearful suffering God** *does* inflict even in this **world! You have** seen some wretched being dying of a disease **that made** him appalling to look at,—that kept him for weeks (I have known it months) in sleepless, unutterable agony:—*Who* kept that wretched being in that unutterable agony? Who, but God! **God, in** His mysterious, unsearchable sovereignty!—

No man would have kept that poor sufferer in that suffering for one minute. But God keeps him there: keeps him day after day, week after week.—Oh, my friends, we have an inflexible Judge to face, merciful though He be ! So pain teaches us something of the severity of God. Now, if you have ever suffered great, unspeakable pain : think ; Here is a glimpse of what it is possible for a human being to suffer : Here is a hint of how dreadfully God *can* punish : Here is a distant glimpse of what perdition may be !

But I turn gladly to another lesson, a far happier lesson, taught us by pain. It reminds us how great was our Blessed Saviour's love for our poor sinful souls, which made Him bear such an unutterable load of anguish as He bore for us.—You know, that we in this world always like to have some standard by which to measure things. Merely to say that a thing is very great and big, fails to convey to us a clear idea : we need to get a standard by which to estimate it, and thus discover *how* great it is. You tell us that it is a long, long way to some far-away place : well, *that* leaves us with rather a vague notion of the distance : but measure it by some standard,—say it is five hundred miles, or a thousand miles off,—and then we know exactly what to think. And we do just the same thing in the world of mind, as in the world of matter ; though of course the standard here is not a material one. You tell us that a man's attachment to his principles, political or religious, is very great.

Well, give us some idea *how* great. What has it led him to do: what to sacrifice: what to suffer? *That* is the test here. **You tell us that a** man's love for some dear friend is deep. How deep? What will it make him **do,** or endure? *That* **is the test. And so, we have a** standard by **which** to estimate the redeeming love of Christ. It "passeth knowledge," indeed: **we must** never forget *that:* its full depth and **intensity reach** beyond our understanding : but this **much about it we can** understand, that it is a love **stronger and** deeper than the deepest and strongest **pain. It has been** tried by *that;* and it stood the **trial!** How great was the Saviour's love for us poor **sinners,—how deep His** desire for our salvation from **sin and** perdition,—we never can fully know : but this **we know, that they sufficed to lead Him, with calm** unflinching **resolution, to** face and to endure pain and anguish so deep **and** crushing, that never **before or** since has their like been **known in this world. Our** Saviour's love for us was stronger than pain, **stronger than agony,** stronger than **death!** It led Him, **perfectly aware of what He** was about to suffer, **to suffer all these. Never was sorrow like His sorrow:** surely **never was love like His love!**

Such, **my hearers, are certain lessons which we are** taught by pain. **But in** the better world, pain will not be needful to enforce them. **They** will be remembered there, so far as it is fit that **they should be** remembered, without the necessity of **having that** sad monitor ever

near. And thus, as in that happy country, pain would
be of no use, pain will go. Useful, gloomily useful, in
this world, it would be of no use there. Its work is
done: and like all other sorrowful things, it shall be
excluded. Oh the comfort of the thought ! Christians,
who have suffered much in this being, remember this,
that in Heaven there shall be " no more pain." And
you, my friends, how stands your interest in this promise ? You have all known pain here : you may have
much more to go through before you quit this world :
how stand your prospects for the country beyond the
grave ? There is a region *there*, where it is all pain
for ever : is there one soul here that will reject the
Saviour's offered love, and face that never-ending pain !
Or rather, when you think of all He bore for you :
when you think of the mercy He freely offers : when
you think of God's solemn declaration, that He is
" not willing that any should perish, but that all
should come to repentance :" where would be your
hearts if you did not feel a responsive love to Him
who so loved you,—a hearty, humble faith and trust
in Him who bids you only trust yourselves to Him ;
and sinful as you are, lost as you are, liable most justly
to endless wrath and punishment as you are, He will
bear you safely through life and death and judgment,
to that better country, where suffering is gone for
ever ;—and, better yet, where sin is done with for ever
too !

And now, as I draw another Sunday's sermon

to an end, I look back once more to my text : I rest in the simple contemplation of the sublime truth which it conveys. "No more pain!" The parting pang which the believer feels in leaving this world, is the very last that he shall ever feel at all. The suffering which he may be called to endure in the closing days of this mortal life, is the very last suffering that he will ever know. The moment in which the last breath is drawn,—in that moment, pain goes for ever! And, it may be, you have seen something which reminded you of that glorious truth, even in the features of the dead face. You have seen, perhaps, the face that had grown old in life, look young after death. You have seen the expression of many years since, lost for long, come out startlingly in the features, fixed and cold. Every one has seen it : and it is sometimes strange how rapidly the change takes place. The marks of pain fade out; and with them the marks of age. I lately saw an aged Christian die. She had borne sharp pain for many days with the endurance of a martyr : she had to bear sharp pain to the very last. The features were tense and rigid with suffering : they remained so while life remained. It was a beautiful sight to see the change which took place in the very instant of dissolution. The features, sharp for many days with pain, in that instant recovered the old aspect of quietude which they had borne in health : the tense, tight look was gone. You saw the signs of pain go out. You felt that all suffering was over. It was no

more of course than the working of physical law : but
in that case it seemed as if there were a further meaning conveyed.   It was hardly possible to look on the
features, so suffering the one moment, so quiet and
calm the next, without remembering words which tell
us, concerning the country into which the believer
enters in the instant of his departure, that *There* " shall
be no more death, neither sorrow, nor crying ; NEITHER
SHALL THERE BE ANY MORE PAIN ! "

XIV.

THE VICTORY OVER THE WORLD.

"And this is the victory that overcometh the world, even our
faith."—1 JOHN v. 4.

THIS text implies and suggests two great lessons:
one of these is that the Christian has to overcome the world,—that there is some sense in which
the world is an enemy, an obstacle, to the Christian,
—an obstacle which must be got over, an enemy
which must be overcome : and the other lesson is that
Faith is the way and the means by which the Christian can and must overcome the world. And when
we look to the first clause of the verse, we find a further truth suggested,—to wit, that this overcoming the
world is a thing of vital and essential concern,—that
it is indeed a test of a professing Christian's profession,
—that if any professing Christian has not overcome
the world, but is manifestly in subjection and bondage
to it, this shews that he is not truly a Christian. For
" whatsoever,"—or perhaps it ought to read " *whosoever* is born of God overcometh the world ; and *this* is
the victory that overcometh the world, even our faith.'

We do not live long before we come to understand,

that it has pleased God so to order things in this life, that no worthy end can be attained without an effort, —without encountering and overcoming opposition. Anything that costs nothing, is generally worth nothing. It is difficult to do anything that is good; and the Christian life is in keeping with all things around it. The schoolboy soon knows that it is difficult to be diligent and industrious,—it is hard work to learn his lessons thoroughly and well;—but it is quite easy to sit idle and do nothing. The farmer knows that he must work early and late to get his field to produce a good crop: while he has only to neglect his field and do nothing, to have it covered with abundance of weeds. The man who wishes to do good, physical or spiritual, to his fellow-men, finds that *that* cannot be done by sitting still in his easy chair and dreaming: he must go forth, and go through work, often rough work, sometimes painful and discouraging work. It is energetic, muscular philanthropy, that purifies the cottage air, and tidies the cottage door, and trains the neglected children. And it is just in religion as it is in everything else. It is difficult to be a true, earnest Christian. It is easy to be a careless, worldly person. Wide is the gate, and broad is the way, that leads to destruction; while we must *strive*,—and Christ's word means more than *strive*,—it means that we must make a strong and agonising effort,—to enter in at the strait gate; and the path of duty, the path to heaven, is an up-hill path. And the text points out one great obstacle, a host of obstacles in itself, in the Christian's heavenward way. The world is in the way. And if we would live the Christian life, if we would reach the Christian's home,—there is no other course,—we must " overcome the world ! "

We are far from saying that the world is the only thing the Christian has to overcome, in his progress towards a better world. There is the great Adversary and Enemy of all good : there is the weak and earthward heart within : but I believe I am expressing the experience of most men who are seeking to lead Christian lives in these days on which we have fallen, when I say that the world is practically the great obstacle to be overcome,—that worldliness is the great besetting sin which most of us have to resist. The cares of the world are in truth the great things that choke the good seed so that it becomes unfruitful. The great thing which most of us have to lament, and confess, and strive against, is, being so occupied and engrossed by our affairs in this world as quite to neglect our preparation for the world beyond the grave. Few Christians in ordinary society and ordinary life are tempted to gross and crying sins : most of us deserve no credit for being free from such, for we have really never been strongly tempted to them. The great thing is just that we are *worldly ;* that we live too much as if this life were all ; that our minds are quite filled with worldly business, worldly pleasure, worldly cares, anxieties, sorrows, losses ; that we are

more anxious about our worldly circumstances, than
about our interest in Christ,—more careful of our
bodily health than of our spiritual,—more set, in short,
(we all know what it means,) upon the seen and temporal than upon the unseen and eternal. Now, my
friends, not only is worldliness a sin, but it is a sin
that chokes all good : it chokes and kills all the fruits
of the Spirit ; and it makes the soul as unfit for
heaven as the grossest crime could. It is our besetting sin : it is our most perilous malady : it concerns
us, with momentous concern, to understand it and
strive against it : and so let us, praying for Divine
direction, look at some of the ways in which the
world is an enemy, an obstacle, a hindrance in our
Christian course ; and let us see how faith is needful
to overcome it.

And, first, this world is an obstacle, needing to be
overcome,—it exerts, that is, an influence which we
must every day be resisting and praying against,—just
in this : that it looks so solid and so real, that in comparison with it, the eternal world and its interests look
to most men as though they had but a shadowy and
unsubstantial existence. And it is a terrible obstacle
this, in our Christian life. No doubt it is for a wise
and good reason that the Almighty suffers it to be so :
but oh how hard it is to feel, day by day, that things
which we cannot see or touch are the most real things
in nature : how hard it is to feel that pardon of sin
and peace with God are more truly the " necessaries

of life" than the daily bread and the nightly shelter,—that a saving interest in Christ's great Atonement is really the "one thing needful!" Oh! it would be well with us if we could only feel as sensibly that we need salvation as that we need food and raiment! Oh! it would be well for us if we could only realise it as strongly, that there is a country beyond the grave, as that there is a country beyond the Atlantic! How many great religious truths,—truths which lie at the foundation of all religion,—we believe in a sadly half-hearted way, because this solid world looks like a constant silent contradiction of them! The supreme importance of the life to come is the doctrine on which all religion rests : but though we often hear and repeat the words, that "all on earth is shadow, all beyond is substance,"—and although sometimes, perhaps in the house of prayer, we may feel our souls lifted up to an elevation from which we discern the fact with a start-ling reality never known on ordinary days of life,—still when the parting hymn is sung, and the benedic-tion pronounced, and we pass out through the church door, and see before us the great hills, and the ancient trees, and feel beneath our feet the solid earth, and hear the voices of people round us,—how fast this world of sense grows and greatens upon us again,—while the unseen world and all its concerns seem to recede into distance, to melt into air, to fade into no-thing! Do you not feel all that, my friends? Do you not feel that this world shuts out, somehow, the next world from your view; and crowds out the next world from your heart!   And what is there that shall "overcome" this materialising influence of a present world: what is there that shall give us the "victory" over it; —but Faith,—Faith which believes what it cannot see, with all the vividness of sight?   Surely, by its very nature, Christian faith, that faith which is wrought in the believing heart by the Blessed Spirit,—is the only thing that can avail us here.   We see and feel this world,—we believe the other: we see and feel the body, and bodily wants,—we believe the soul and its necessities: oh that by God's grace faith may be made to vanquish sight,—it never will vanquish sight as we might wish it should,—but at least vanquish sight and sense in so far as that it shall be the guide of our conduct,—as that we shall act according to the dictates of faith,—as that we shall live and act according to what we believe and not according to what we see ;—and thus that, like the apostle, we shall "walk by faith and not by sight !"   It is too much, perhaps, to expect that the day should ever come, when, for more than short seasons of special elevation, we shall be able to realise the unseen and eternal as plainly as we do the seen and temporal: we cannot look to be always so raised above worldly interests, as to feel that not what we grasp, but what we believe, is the true reality: it will be enough if we carry with us such a conviction as shall constrain us to "seek *first* the kingdom of God and His righteousness:" and if we ever do so, *this* must be "the **victory** which shall overcome the world, even our faith."

So far, then, for one respect in which faith is needful to resist an influence of the world, hostile to our spiritual life : and next we remark that the world **is an** obstacle in our Christian course, because its cares, business, interests, tend strongly and directly to choke the good seed of religion in the heart,—to fill up our minds so completely as that they shall have no room **for** thoughts of eternity and salvation. Oh how many notable housewives, busy from morning till night with their household affairs, their children, their servants, could tell us that they scarce can find a minute to read **the Bible, or to stop** and think where they are going ; and that at morning they are so anxious to get to the avocations of the day, and at evening so completely wearied and worn out, that they have not time nor heart for prayer. How many a toiling, anxious man, working and scheming to make the ends meet, and to maintain his children, and to advance them in life, has **not a** thought to spare for the other world ;—for his own **soul's eternal** destiny, or for the eternal destiny of **those he** holds **dear !** It is when we are " careful and troubled about many things," that we are ready to forget that " one thing is needful." I need not tell you that in all ages of the Church, every man who has earnestly tried to lead a Christian life, has felt, more or less, how great an obstacle earthly care has ever been.

You know how, in centuries past, men have tried to evade this world instead of overcoming it,—to fly from the enemy instead of facing and vanquishing it: how they have left the world behind them, and sought in the monastic shade a retreat to which worldly care should never come,—a home where the turmoil and strife should never be heard, save softened by the distance into a murmur that would but lull the ear. Ah, it was a vain endeavour: but still it proved how great an enemy of spiritual life worldly care was felt to be, —when, only to be rid of it, men were found willing to give up almost everything that human hearts hold dear! How many a time have you knelt down in your closet to say your evening prayer; and in a little while found that some worldly anxiety or trouble was coming between you and your God;—that your thoughts were wandering away upon your earthly cares, and would not leave you undistracted even for the little time given to devotion! How often in the house of prayer, the words of exhortation fell effectless and unnoted on your ear, because your thoughts were away about the cares you had left at home,—about how you were to find the money which you *must* have by a certain day, or about the pale cheek and the failing strength of your little sickly child! Oh, how shall we overcome these things, my Christian friends? How shall we keep these worldly cares which we cannot escape, from making our souls utterly worldly? How can it be brought to this, that the man in business may give to his business just thought enough and no more, —that the parent may not let his children's welfare come between him and his salvation,—that " care's unthankful gloom " may not nip all holy affections and aspirations, and make us worn, miserable, anxious creatures, wretched in time, but not able to spare a thought for eternity? Only the " faith that overcometh the world " can save from this. Only that child-like confidence in our Saviour's love and wisdom and power, which trusts everything to Him,—which " casts all our care upon Him " and His strong arm,—and so feels the crushing burden lifted from our own weak hearts ! " *This* is the victory that overcometh,"—the only thing that ever can overcome,—" the world ;— even our faith !" What we need, to overcome worldly care, is *that* faith which lifts its head above the atmo- sphere of time, into eternity's clearer light ! What we need is faith to realise how short this life is, when compared with the great eternity : how little and how fleeting are all worldly interests, all earthly gains and losses, when compared with the pearl of great price, an assured part in Christ's great salvation. What we need is faith to realise that no earthly end or aim should be regarded as our " chief end ;" and that every earthly thing has yielded us the best it can give, when it has wrought together towards our immortal welfare ! What we need is faith to feel that the true riches lie not in broad acres nor in hoarded wealth, from which a week's illness or a moment's shock may part us for ever;—but in that nobler estate which is garnered up within the soul,—those " treasures laid up in heaven, which neither moth nor rust can corrupt, and which no thief can break through and steal !" Give us *that* faith ; and we *have* " overcome the world :" it is our tyrant, and we are its slaves, no more ! Give us *that* faith, not for isolated moments of rapture only, but to be the daily mood and temper of our hearts : and then we shall engage without fever in the business of this world, as feeling that in a few short years it will matter nothing whether we met disappointment or success : then we shall seek for wealth, if we seek at all, as those who remember that in a very little we are going where we shall never be asked whether we were rich or poor : then we shall feel, that once safe in Christ, nothing can go amiss with us,—that God has undertaken' for us,—and that it is His concern and not ours to arrange and dispose all the events of our worldly lot. And shall we not thus " overcome the world :" break from its thousand ties, cast off its downward gravitation,—break away from its control, free and untrammelled, as the lion that bounds scatheless from the hunter's net ! Be it our prayer, then, when we think how soul-destroying a thing worldly care is in its own nature, that God, of His abundant grace, may vouchsafe to each and all of us " the victory that overcometh the world,—even *such* faith !"

It is too much to ask of frail human beings, merely to remove their affections from the things of time and sense. It will not do, merely to tell us that we are not to "love this world," unless you point out to us what we are to love instead. We cannot turn away from this world, evil though it be ; when we turn our back upon *it*, we see but a blank before us. And here it is that all systems but Christianity have failed, when they sought to teach men how they might rise superior to worldly concerns, and thus "overcome the world." It was easy to shew that the things which are seen can never make us happy : easy to repeat the moral lesson that it was foolish to give the heart to what can stand us in so little stead : but it was useless to advise man to set his affection and lay up his treasure nowhere : and it is faith only which can apprehend and lay hold of the things which are not seen. It is the faith which holds in view another world, which alone can overcome this : can overlook it, as the eye, that rests on mountains far away, over-looks the fields that lie between. The soul that is accustomed to gaze on spiritual and eternal things, sees earthly objects in their real insignificance : and to see this world as it truly is, is to overcome it. It is like the embodied demons of classic fable, who fled if you did but recognise and name them. Estimate this world,—as faith alone estimates it, at its true worth ; and in that act you have "overcome the world !"

There is yet another sense in which the world is an

obstacle to our Christian life, needing to be overcome by faith. As you know, the phrase *the World* is sometimes used in contrast with *the Church :* so our Saviour used it all through his Intercessory Prayer ; as when He said of His disciples, "They are not of the world, even as I am not of the world." Taken in this way, *the World* means all human beings who are without the Christian fold : who are devoid of Christian faith, and of Christian ways of thinking and feeling. And you know well that on the most important subjects there is an absolute contrariety between the doctrines of the church and of the world : and many a believer has found the world's frown or the world's sneer something which it needs much faith to resist and to overcome. Perhaps in the case of most of *us*, living among those who make a profession of Christianity, or who at least respectfully recognise it, this opposition is but little felt : and probably in the case of hardly any is it such as in past days it has been. Yet it is felt still, by the poor school-boy, sent out from a pious home into that stormy little world, who is afraid to say his prayers lest his companions should laugh at him : and by the poor servant, admitted to some great establishment, who is just as much afraid as her betters of the jeer of some flippant fool, who thinks all seriousness hypocrisy : and by many a youth, sent into circles and professions, where anything like earnestness for his soul's salvation would be met by banter and ridicule, or by the stare of well-bred contempt. It is not everywhere and at all times easy to say practically, "I am not ashamed of the gospel of Christ." There are many professing Christians, who at some tables and in some societies, sink their Christianity for the time. But how *this* opposition crumbles down in the presence of earnest faith ! How easily *that* faith, which realises things spiritual and unseen, overcomes and puts down *this* hostile influence of the world ! How cheaply and lightly will that man hold ridicule and mockery of him and his religion, who realises to his heart that the All-wise and Almighty God thinks upon *that* subject as he does : who realises that God approves the course he follows, whether man does or no : and who can feel that even as the brainless scoffer is raising the laugh at his expense, and the empty circle joins in the derision, a silent Eye looks down approvingly upon what he does, and a pen which the by-standers do not see is registering the "well-done, good and faithful servant !" Ah, make *that* be realised by earnest faith ; and the bonds of this world's fear turn to the strong heart as the green withs were to Samson's nervous arms !

In these senses, then, which have been pointed out, the World is an obstacle in the Christian's way, —an obstacle which he must resist and overcome. Its solid, sensible reality, makes spiritual things look in the comparison shadowy and unreal. Its cares and anxieties choke the word,—engross the soul to the exclusion of all thought of religion. Its maxims and its fear, " the world's dread laugh," tend sometimes to make the disciple of Christ ashamed of his Christian profession and his Divine Master. And over all these hostile influences faith gives us the victory; and nothing but faith can. You may tell me, indeed, that there have been men, who had no Christian faith, and who made no pretence of it, who yet have appeared wonderfully dead to this world's power, and who sat very loosely to the things of time and sense. And if it were to " overcome the world," merely to turn away from it in disgust ;—if he can be said to have " overcome the world," who has broken away from all the ties by which it maintains its hold on human hearts,—who has grown " weary of the sun," and sick of all ambition,—who flies the society of his race, and scorns its opinions,—*then* indeed it would be hard to shew that Christian faith in the heart is the only thing that can " overcome the world." Rather in that case we might say, that " This is the victory that overcometh the world, even "—disappointed ambition, blighted affection, shattered nerves, frustrated anticipations and hopes. Rather in that case should we point to the sated voluptuary, the betrayed politician, the solitary misanthrope,—than to the Christian, genial, kind, and true. Rather in that case should we have to seek the hero, victorious over time and sense, where the lonely waves made sad music round the cynic man-hater's dwelling, or where the poet's genius has shewn us the desolate wanderer, wearied of all he felt, or heard, or saw. But *that*, my brethren, is not conquering the world : it is succumbing to the world : it is letting the world conquer us ! It is not to overcome the world, merely to take the pet at it, like a spoiled child, because it will not let us have our own way. In all these cases, the moody dejection which marks him who has thus turned his back upon the world, testifies that the world has still its hold upon his heart ; and that if the present cloud were but removed, if times of prosperity came back, he would return to earthly pursuits and follies with as keen a relish as ever. We look with suspicion upon him who professes that he has renounced the world, just when the world has renounced *him:* who lays down the empty cup, and says the draught is bitter : who declares that the objects of earthly ambition are vanity—but not till he has found that they lie beyond his reach. No doubt sorrows and disappointments are sometimes the sharp discipline by which God weans His children's hearts from worldly things : no doubt the path of tribulation sometimes serves to quicken our steps towards the kingdom of God : no doubt experience of the insufficiency of earthly things to make us happy, oftentimes tends to turn us to that Blessed Saviour who alone can give peace and rest to our weary souls : and in this way all worldly troubles may be used by the Holy Spirit as means for working in us that faith which overcomes the world. But it is not mere sorrow that overcomes the world : nor is it sorrow left to its own natural results. Sorrow by itself tends merely to crush us down : it brings us to the earth, rather than raises us above it : it was natural in Job, in his time of great desolation, to "fall down upon the ground :" but faith takes the further step, and raises the affections from things on earth to things in heaven. Sorrow is in itself an idle thing : it leaves us no heart to do anything : yet God's Spirit, from that unpromising source, sometimes draws forth that energetic faith, which "purifieth the heart, and worketh by love, and overcometh the world." And then, after the sorrow is gone, its happy results remain : the Saviour, whose preciousness was found in the night of weeping, is still found precious when the night has passed away : the lesson learned under the heavy discipline of sorrow, is remembered and acted upon when happier days return : and the soul, emancipated from the trammels of the world, acknow- ledges how good it was to be thus afflicted. A saving and permanent change, visible in the whole life, is sometimes left by the season of tribulation : and then, indeed, the world *has* been overcome, when a calm resignation to all the appointments of God's good will,—a resignation which is calm but not apathetic, —has taken the place of that feverish anxiety about worldly things to which we are all so prone. And so, the parent, who has lost his beloved child, has sometimes been able to testify that a blessed lesson was taught him by that little grave : that the removal of that dear one reminded him sharply of what he was forgetting, that *this* is not our rest or our home ; and made one tie more to that happy place, where there is no sin nor sorrow.

And now, as a practical conclusion to my discourse, let me ask each of you whether you have overcome the world. " Whatsoever is born of God overcometh the world :" it is a searching test this : for it means that he who has not overcome the world has not been born of God. It means that if a man be entirely worldly in heart and life, he can be no believer. How is it with *us*, then ? Do we feel most interest in the things of time and sense ? Do we give more time and thought to our worldly work, or to the great employment of working out our salvation ? Are we more anxious to be holy, humble disciples of Jesus, than to get comfortably on through life ? Ah, brethren, answer these questions to yourselves : these are matters which lie between you and God. *He* knows what your answer should be !

We read in history, my friends—what school-boy has not heard of it ?—of one in departed days who fancied that he had accomplished that hard task, which the Apostle John tells us can be accomplished only by him who hath been born of God. We read how he carried his victorious arms over **every** region of the then known earth : **how he** subjugated king after king, and brought nation **after nation** beneath his sway ; **and then** fancied that he **had** " overcome the world !" We read how **he felt it sad to** think that his heroic task was done ; **and** how he wept **that** there **were no more worlds to conquer.** Oh, far **astray,** far mistaken ! There was one world **to** conquer **yet, to** which that conqueror was a **slave : a world** to over-come which the arms of Alexander were of no avail a world that can enslave the man who fancies he has conquered it,—can bind his soul in fetters, and hold in captivity every feeling and thought. **And** *that* world there is but one thing which can conquer. Quietly fought, and fought year after year, **this battle** is fought and won in the humble believer's heart : " and *this* is the victory that overcometh the world, **even our faith !"**

XV.

THE LIMITS OF HUMAN EXPERIENCE.

"There hath no temptation taken you but such as is common
to man."—1 COR. x. 13.

A VERY great number of people firmly believe,
that there never were in this world such people
as themselves: and that nobody ever did what they
have done, or came through what they have come
through. There is in almost every human being, and
in none more decidedly than the most commonplace,
a lurking belief that there never was such a being as
himself. You will find this especially in the narrower,
and less cultivated minds: and in them it often
appears in forms which are irritating and ridiculous.
You will find folk who really believe that they themselves, and all their belongings, are much better than
other folk, and *their* belongings: that there never
were such children as theirs; that there never were
such flowers and vegetables as theirs; that there
never were such toils as theirs; and even (for there is
no reckoning the odd ways in which human vanity
will gratify itself) that there never were such headaches
and such worries as theirs. All this comes of a

morbid self-conceit. It is just the person who is
below the average of the race, who will fancy that he
stands above all his fellow-creatures. And all this
goes rather to constitute one of those weaknesses
which should be touched by the moralist, than to
rank among those graver matters of doctrine and
practice which are to be specially thought of in the
house of prayer.

But there is a particular manifestation of the same
tendency in fallen human nature, against which an
apostle thought it worth while solemnly to caution his
friends in an epistle inspired by the Holy Spirit; and
which well deserves the most earnest consideration
which can be given it upon this day and in this place.
This tendency in each human soul to single itself out
from the mass of mankind, does not always appear in
those self-conceited and unamiable forms to which we
have alluded. It sometimes manifests itself in forms
of feeling and belief which deserve our heartiest
sympathy: it often prompts human beings to write
hard things against themselves, and to esteem themselves as parted from others, not by being better but
by being worse. Every minister often meets with
people who, having been deeply convinced of their
sinfulness, and of their lost estate by nature, run into
an extreme which for the time threatens to drive
them to despair. They fancy that there never were
such sinners as they are: that they have sinned
beyond hope: that not even Christ's blood can wash

away such sins as theirs: that there never were such evil thoughts as have passed through their hearts: that there never were transgressions so aggravated and so black as theirs: that all the gracious words of scripture you can remind them of, apply to other people but not to them: that you may just leave them alone, as past all redemption. Then you will find others who have got past this mournful and distressing stage: who have been brought to commit their souls to Christ, and who have found some little measure of hope and peace, but who seem likely to be desponding pilgrims to the end. They *will* have it that there never were believers so weak as they are: never Christians with so little heart for duty: never Christians so little equal to face the toils, perils, temptations of the way: and never such temptations, toils, and perils as those which they must pass through. And in such cases as those I have been describing, there is nothing of that silly vanity which has been spoken of: instead of being vain of being different from others, the fancied pre-eminence in sin and sorrow is a cause of deep and unaffected anguish: and such poor souls would be thankful if you could but assure and convince them that they fare no worse than millions have fared before them: that they share just the common lot of the race. It was to such people as these, that St Paul wrote the words of the text. They were pressed by many temptations, these Christians of Corinth: and forasmuch as human nature is in its essence always the same, we may well believe that they were sometimes ready to despair, and to fancy that never were believers pressed so hard. And so St Paul **assures** them, in words which would doubtless be felt as affording strong consolation, that it was to them just **as it had been to others.** He says, "There hath no temptation taken *you*, but such as is common to man."

The Apostle, you see, speaks of Temptation: but without **the least** straining, **we may** understand the text as reaching to much more than *that.* **It is not** temptation **alone** which **we** share with **our** race: but cares, sorrows, and bereavements too: **in short, all** that makes the common lot of human - kind. **We** fancy, when painful trials come to ourselves, **that** things so painful were never felt before: **we feel trial** so sharply when it touches ourselves: **we cannot** help its being so. **But** our text reminds us that there **is a** limit, within which all human experience **lies. Human** ability, and human endurance: **what man can do,** and what man can suffer: all these things have their tether, and **cannot range very far. Here is a lesson** of humility for the self-conceited, who fancy that there never were people **so clever** or so wise or so laborious **as** themselves: let them remember that **thousands** more have been at least as good. **Here is comfort** for those bowed down under the sense **of** sinfulness, and thinking that the human being **never breathed** **who had so** provoked God's wrath and **so wearied**

God's forbearance : thousands are now in heaven who **once** thought all *that,* and who have sinned as deeply **as** they. Here is encouragement for the tempted, ready to faint and fail : thousands more have felt the like, and by God's grace have been led safely through **it.** There **is** nothing in our powers, our circumstances, our sufferings, our merits, our sins, our temptations, **but** what lies within the reach of human experience : we are but treading the track which wiser and **better** men have trodden before us : "There hath nothing befallen *us,* but such as is common to man !"

So you see, my friends, that the thought suggested **in** the text may be useful as a medicine for two spiritual diseases most opposite to one another in nature. You know that the two opposite errors to which believers are tempted, **as** regards mood and feeling, are Presumption, **and** Despair. We may think of ourselves too highly : we may judge ourselves too safe : **we** may fancy that we are quite equal to all the duty **and** the temptation that can come our way. *That* is **the error** upon one hand : *that* is presumption. And **the vain** self-conceit which prompts to it meets **its** rebuke **in the** assurance that we are no whit wiser, or better, **or safer,** than other men : and **as we all** know how other men have failed and fallen, we may well stand in fear lest we should do the like ; and we may well feel our simple dependence upon grace from above ; and seek it and look for it earnestly and daily. **But the** pendulum swings as far to the left, as it had previously swung to the right: and as presumption lies at the extremity on one side, so despair lies at the extremity on the other: and although down-hearted and desponding believers are oftentimes so almost ceaselessly, still we all know, too, that believers sometimes pass all of a sudden from the one extreme to the other: and you will find people who within a few days or hours will pass through the most diverse and inconsistent spiritual moods: at one time fancying that their sins are beyond those of all other sinners, and at another that their attainments are above those of almost all other believers. Now we know that though God disapproves Presumption, he also disapproves its opposite, Despair: and the dis-trust of God, and the exaggerated sense of our own sinfulness and weakness, which lead to Despair, find their remedy in the self-same text which rebuked Presumption,—in the assurance that great as is our guilt, the blood of Christ has washed white souls as guilty: that great as is our weakness, Christians as weak have been enabled by God's Spirit to tread to the end a path as rough and steep as ours can be: and that manifold as are our temptations, they are no unexampled temptations;—that others have felt them all;—that "there hath no temptation taken *us*, but such as is common to man."

My friends, it is to the comforting view of the text, and not to the humbling one, that I wish at this time to direct your thoughts. It was as comfort that St

Paul addressed this text to the Corinthians. He did not mean to take them down by it; but to encourage them. They had not reached that morbid stage, that they were proud of their troubles, and given to boast about them. The text is addressed to such as feel their troubles and temptations far too deeply and really for *that.* And let us, this day, for our own comfort and encouragement in our pilgrimage course, dwell for a little upon the assurance in the text, regarded in its comforting aspect. Doubtless there are in this congregation some who need all the comfort the text can yield: and let us humbly ask that the Blessed Spirit would convey its strong consolation to their hearts.

And the first case which suggests itself as one in which the text may afford comfort, is, when the soul is brought under the deep conviction of sin. You know, my friends, that if you wish to persuade a sick man to send for the physician, the first thing you must do is to convince him that he *is* sick. It is just an application of that principle of plain common sense, that in order to get a man to take pains to get anything, you must get him to see that he needs it, and that he cannot do without it. Now Christianity, in all that part of it which human minds can understand, is essentially a common-sense scheme. And the Holy Spirit, in leading men to believe in Christ, acts upon plain principles, which we can all see to be the right ones. The Holy Spirit begins His saving work upon a careless human soul: see how He works.

He wishes to lead the careless soul to the Great Physician of souls: He begins, accordingly, by shewing the careless soul how sick it is. He wishes to lead the man to labour and strive to find pardon and peace with God: He begins, accordingly, by shewing the man how much he needs pardon and peace with God. He wishes us to go to the Saviour of sinners: He begins, by convincing us that we are sinners, and so that we need a Saviour. Now, there is no doubt, there is something very startling in the first deep conviction that we are sinners. It is so new. It is something quite strange. It is a conviction quite different from that which we entertained before. For the natural thing is, to think that we are not very great sinners: that we have never done very many sins; and that those which we have done are not so very bad. And when God's Spirit convinces us of sin: makes us really feel the sober truth of the confessions of sin which we utter in our prayers without at all meaning them: makes us really discern the tremendous risk in which we stand of that fearful doom whose mention is so often the profane man's jest: then the soul is sometimes ready to run from the one extreme, of Presumption, to the other extreme, of Despair: and to pass from an easy-going indifference as to its salvation, to an anxiety so urgent and terrible as has sometimes threatened to overthrow reason itself. And doubtless, this is a sad and dark stage to pass through: if there be any within these

walls now passing through it, to such we would say, dark and sad as it is, it is far better than the reckless indifference which went before it: Be thankful that you are unhappy: the Holy Spirit has not left you: **He is** making you feel that you are under the disease; **and never** fear but He will by and by lead you **to the remedy for it.** The truly hopeless symptom in the **case of the** unconverted man, is when he knows he is **unconverted, and** does not care at all. But, brethren, one of the most common feelings of the soul awakened **to a sense of sin,** is, that there never was sin like its **own.** From fancying that he is hardly a sinner at all, the man goes to the other extreme, and fancies that **there never was** such a sinner in the world. It is not in every case that this is so: but assuredly it is so in a very great number of cases. **And** deep as is the soul's distress in that sad time, deep as is its sense of sinfulness, it would be unspeakable comfort if you could only persuade it that other men have felt **the** like; and that others have had the self-same crushing conviction of sin. No doubt, the feeling is a morbid **one, which** prompts any one to say, " I have sinned **as no other ever** sinned: I fear I am beyond hope, so aggravated has been my guilt: all that you can say of God's mercy and **the** Redeemer's blood may give comfort to **others,** but not **to me."** The feeling that prompts such words is a morbid **one,** indeed: but **it is a** common one: **It is just a** manifestation of the great fact in our nature, that what touches ourselves comes home to us as nothing else can : and you will find people, sharp enough at discerning the folly of such a feeling in the case of others, who when the Spirit brings sin home to themselves, evince it all. Now it may be difficult to explain why, but it is quite certain that there is something re-assuring and comforting in being really made to believe that we are no worse off than others : in being really made to feel that all this trouble we are passing through is nothing untried and unprecedented : that we are journeying along no untrodden way, but along a path beaten by the feet of multitudes more. Oh that I could even now carry it home to any, burdened down with the sense of sin, that many who are now thankful and happy believers, that many who are now in heaven, have had the self-same fears, and have seen their sins in the very same way ! Oh that I could carry it to the despairing heart, that there is no sin but Christ's blood can wash away : that He did not come to save those who fancied they really do not need much saving, but " to save sinners, even the chief :" that it is a hopeful sign that we shall find the Physician of souls, when we feel how sorely we are stricken with the disease : and that sinfulness, in its very darkest manifestations, is nothing other than a disease " which is common to man !"

A second case in which the text may afford comfort, is that which the Apostle had especially in his mind, when he wrote it: it is in the prospect and under the pressure of temptation. My friends, apart from any reason which would bear logical scrutiny, there is comfort under any trouble in the bare thought that other human beings have known the like trouble; that we are treated no more hardly than our fellow-men. But as regards temptation, our text suggests more than merely this undefined and comparatively sentimental consolation: we can draw comfort under temptation from our text by stern logic, as well as through the medium of a kind of vague emotional impulse. For we may soundly argue, that if no temptation is likely to assail us, except temptation through which human souls as weak as we have by God's grace passed safely into glory,—then that we too may hope, by the same blessed aid, to fight our way through all the influences which would lead towards ruin, till we enter on the holiness, the safety, the rest above. That which man has done, man may do. The great adversary, and the ensnaring world, fairly vanquished in a hundred battles, may well be vanquished again. No doubt, we may imagine temptations which would be too much for human beings to resist; and duties too weighty for human beings to do: but, if we be true believers, we have God's word for it, that such shall not come our way. There is a limit, beyond which the strength of any impulse to sin shall not be suffered to reach: and though the great Adversary and Tempter may go about continually seeking whom he may deceive and mislead, after all, he fights in fetters ;—there is a point· beyond which his power and craft shall never be allowed to reach ;—and *that* is the point up to which each one of us may, by honest effort on our own part, and by God's directing and sustaining grace, fairly resist and vanquish him. Temptation may indeed often come, which the man who does not honestly want to resist it may be willing to fancy irresistible : it is not a half-hearted opposition that will suffice to put temptation down : and in too many instances, we are, all, but too anxious to persuade ourselves that under pressure so strong as that which is bearing upon us, we should be more than human if we did not deviate somewhat from the strict line of right. When you meet some malignant injury, there is a strong provocation to bitterness and revenge : when you are passed over in favour of one you may think less deserving than yourself, there is a strong provocation to envy, discontent, murmuring against God : when you have the opportunity of acquiring profit by means which are unfair and dishonest, but which you know quite well that many reputable people would not for a moment hesitate to employ, there is a strong temptation to stifle the voice of conscience and of God's Spirit, and to do that unfair thing. But in every such case, you know thoroughly well, that though temptation was strong, it was not by any means overwhelming : you could have resisted it if you had honestly tried: and the reason why you yielded to it was not that temptation was irresistible, but that inclination lay that way. You know perfectly well, that for the evil you have done, even under that pressure, you are justly responsible to God. And you would not feel that you were thus responsible, if you could truly say at God's judgment-seat, that before Him you could not choose but do the evil you have done: that you were powerless in the hand of temptation, and could but drift before it as a ship before the overmastering hurricane. So you see there is a double lesson in our text for those subjected to temptation. There is comfort; and there is caution. If you honestly and truly wish to go on in God's way, there is abounding comfort. There is the comfort, that though manifold temptations will strive to lead you wrong,—though many siren voices may whisper evil to your heart, and many weighty considerations may tend towards profitable and pleasant sin,—and though a whole array of crafty spirits may plot your downfall, and though their dark, malignant Ruler be ever near: —still that the temptation will never come that would need angelic strength to resist: the temptation will never come that human beings like ourselves have not faced already; and which God's grace and our own faithful endeavours will not enable us to pass through. But there is the caution too; that if you are an insincere and half-hearted Christian, seeking to just reach heaven at last after having held by the world

here, you need never think to cloak your own prone-
ness to go astray under the pretext that temptation
overpowered you. Never think, as some hypocritically do, to cast wholly upon Satan the sin into which
they went quite readily themselves. You will find
people who will utter phrases of hateful cant which
seem to imply that it is Satan's fault they have done
wrong; and that it is really no concern of theirs. Ah
brethren, when a man sins, the sin is essentially his
own. He must answer for it himself. Satan might
tempt him to do wrong; but Satan could not compel
him to do wrong: his own evil heart must have con-
sented to the evil he has done. Satan is bad enough:
but some people would hypocritically give him credit
for things with which he has very little to do. I know,
my hearers, that cases may be supposed in which
temptation may be regarded as truly overwhelming.
I know that the starving man would be punished
neither by man nor by God for taking the bread which
is to save him from death by famine: but *that* case is
almost the only supposable one in which in actual life
temptation ever becomes truly irresistible: and such
cases we may very fitly leave to the Divine justice and
mercy. I know that even human law admits that
strong provocation may diminish responsibility though
it do not destroy it: and we may be sure that all the
principles of right and justice will not be forgot by
God. But the believer has a sure promise,—which
the worldly man has not,—that all overwhelming

extremes of temptation shall be warded off from him. For how speaks the Apostle, in the words which follow those of the text? "God is faithful, who will not suffer you to be tempted above that ye are able : but will with the temptation also make a way to escape, that ye may be able to bear it."

The last case which I shall mention as one in which the text may speak comfort, is under great sorrow : under bereavement, or trial of any kind. I am not forgetting how beautifully it has been said that in bereavement there is no consolation here. You remember how the greatest of living poets speaks of the fashion in which some tried to comfort him under the loss of his dearest friend :—

> One writes, that "other friends remain,"—
> That "loss is common to the race :"—
> And common is the commonplace,
> And vacant chaff well meant for grain.
>
> That loss is common would not make
> My own less bitter, rather more ;
> Too common ! Never morning wore
> To evening, but some heart did break.

I know, brethren, that it may be said heartlessly : but even in the face of the poet's lines, I say there is comfort in sorrow, when it is rightly regarded, in the truth that " there hath nothing befallen us but such as is common to man." Surely even the thought that we have companions in sorrow,—that those who have felt the like can feel for us, and understand our distress, and sympathise with us,—has in it something of comfort. I think that the mother who has lost her child, would feel a consolation, hard perhaps to define, when another, who has passed through the like trial, does but come and sit by her, and say no word but that she has felt the same. Surely there is something consoling to our heart amid our earthly sorrows, in the bare remembrance that our Saviour understands them, because He has felt them all! But the text suggests comfort which may appear to some as more substantial than this. It suggests to us not merely this vague relief: not merely that amid our deepest and freshest grief there is encouragement in the sight of others who have now in so far got over the like,—who have tamed their sorrow,—who have found that grief is transitory no less than joy, and that though it may not leave us what we were, still it leaves us;—but the text suggests too that others who have known such sorrow as we feel, have been enabled by God's grace to bear it, and profit by it, and learn from it, and be sanctified by it; and surely there is something in *that* thought, which should enable us to bow the more submissively to our Heavenly Father's will. I say there is comfort in the remembrance, that the best and noblest of the race have felt all we feel: that through like tribulation the souls in glory have "entered into the kingdom of God:" that the best hearts that ever beat have known the pang of sorrow and bereavement;—that the best

of the race have bent over the freshly-covered grave;
—ay, and gone back to the world to be the better,
kinder, and nobler, for the sad discipline they had
gone through! Others have known it: others have
borne it bravely: others have been sanctified by it:
others have been prepared for glory by it; and so may
we. Yes, this thought is a commonplace: and better
so. It would not be true if it were not. It would
not be level to our understanding and our sympathy,
if it were something new that people had to find out,
after human beings have been sinning and sorrowing
for near six thousand years. I say there is comfort,
real and deep, in thinking that the path of sorrow we
tread, has been beaten smooth and wide by the feet
of the best that ever trod this world: that our Blessed
Saviour was a Man of Sorrows: and that the best of
His Church have been suffered to journey by no other
path than that their Master went. It is not alone,
that the mourner travels through this vale of tears:
Apostles and Prophets are of the company: Saints
and Martyrs go with him: and the sorrowful face of
the Great Redeemer, though sorrowful now no more,
remains for ever with the old look of brotherly sympathy to His servants' eyes and hearts. Nothing hath
come to us: nothing will come to us: but has been
shared by better men. Search out the human being
suffering the sharpest sorrow: and we can match it, in
the best of the Church of God. We fancy, in our
dark days, that no other heart ever felt what we feel:

there was a man who directed that when he was buried, his gravestone should bear no record of his name or history; but just the single word *Miserrimus:* Most Wretched: and he sleeps under the pavement of one of the great Cathedrals of England, with that one word to mark the place. You see *there*, my friends, the natural feeling which you yourselves have known: but you may be sure it is wrong. It is not now, after the tribulation of all these ages, that any human soul can reach that sad pre-eminence! God sanctify sorrow to us, as He has sanctified it to others! They trod the path we tread: and we may humbly hope that it will conduct us to the rest in which they are dwelling. And meanwhile, be sure of this; you who have lately known deep sorrow, you who have bent over the grave where your dearest was laid to sleep the long sleep till the Resurrection day: that nothing has come to you but what God can comfort under, that nothing has come to you but what God can hallow into precious blessing: because there hath nothing befallen you, but what the Wisest and Kindest has seen meet to suffer, shall be common to fallen man!

XVI.

THE PERSONALITY AND AGENCY OF EVIL SPIRITS.

"Your adversary the Devil, as a roaring lion, walketh about, seeking whom he may devour."—1 PETER v. 8.

"And the angels which kept not their first estate, but left their own habitation, he hath reserved in everlasting chains under darkness unto the judgment of the great day."—JUDE 6.

"Depart from me, ye cursed, into everlasting fire, prepared for the Devil and his angels."—ST MATT. xxv. 41.

YOU know, my friends, that when an army is on active service, there is no effort which its commander will spare, to get accurate information about the army which is opposed to him. He uses all the means in his power: he undergoes great fatigues, and his agents and emissaries are content to run the most fearful risks; that he may learn what is the number of the force arrayed against him; what is its position, what its probable movements. And if any skilful spy could so far penetrate the councils of the hostile commander, as to be able to procure a sketch of his plan for conducting the campaign, we can all understand that such a plan would be worth almost any price. For to be forewarned is to be forearmed;

and if you know exactly what are the tactics which are to be employed against you, it will be comparatively easy to evade them.

And, without any minute acquaintance with military matters, we all know that one of the things which a skilful general takes pains to do, is to organise such a system of spies and the like, as may keep him always well-informed of the position, strength, and possible movements of his enemies. Thus he makes sure, so far as may be, that he shall never be taken by surprise. And we can all understand that he would be a very unwise and unskilful commander, who should make up his mind that he did not want to know anything at all about his adversaries: about how many of them there might be: about the time when they might choose to attack him: about the point on which they might make their attack: about the particular kind of attack they might make. And if the military commander, in addition to closing his eyes and ears against all warning as to the host of foes that were waiting to swoop down upon him, were occasionally to allude to them, and the risks he ran from them, as forming an excellent jest: if he brought those around him to this point, that it was an understood thing that there was something essentially ludicrous in the mention of the name of these powerful and crafty foes, so that every silly creature who only managed to introduce their name into his common speech should be regarded as having said

something **smart and witty :** I think you will agree
. that an army so guided and commanded would be in
the sure way to defeat, and disgrace, and destruction.

And yet, my friends, it is hardly necessary to tell
you, that it is precisely in that fashion that **very many
human beings are** accustomed **to treat the most
skilful, crafty,** malignant, **and it may be** numerous
army of foes, that ever **has been** arrayed against God
or man. It is a part of our religious belief, that a
host of beings, with **power and** skill far **more than
human, are daily and hourly exerting all** their power
and all their skill for an end which is no other and no
less than our eternal ruin : it is not the defeat which
one mortal army would inflict upon another, **that they
desire to** inflict **upon us :** the thing which they wish
and work to bring **upon us,** is our eternal misery, and
sin, and shame. **It is part of** our religious belief,
that at the head **of this host of** foes **there is one**
miserable, yet powerful **being :** a being **inconceivably
malignant, crafty,** powerful, wretched : **whose** great
desire is to dishonour God, and to make **us poor
human beings as sinful** and as wretched **as** himself :
our " adversary the Devil, **who,** as **a roaring** lion,
walketh **about,** seeking whom **he may devour."** And
we are taught, **too,** that this blasted **being is** the head
and leader of **an army of** spirits, once pure and
happy, but now **wicked and** wretched, who, under the
darkness of God's wrath, **and** with powers somewhat
limited by the chains of God's will, with no ray of

hope before them in the blank, desolate Eternity, are acting as the Devil's emissaries for human temptation and destruction, and doing all they can to lead us downward to those everlasting fires prepared for him and them. Oh what a dreary, awful picture is sketched out by those three passages of Scripture which I read to you as my text! What despair for our adversaries; what peril, what warning for ourselves! And how, then, do you think it would strike a stranger, if we were to tell him that multitudes of men, assailed every moment by that black army, do practically shut their eyes to the fact · never take the slightest pains to learn anything abou. the power and the wiles of their worst enemies : nay, are so far from seriously understanding and feeling the force of all this which they believe, that the mention of beings, or of a being, so miserable, so awful, so tremendously energetic, active, cunning, malignant, is regarded by some men as a very amusing thing : as giving point to a jest which has little other point: as a signal, whenever it is introduced, for the empty laughter of the fool! Oh surely a subject of such horror; and the contemplation of so much depravity and such unutterable misery ; could never be regarded as matter of amusement and jesting, unless by souls blinded and misled by the wiles of the dark Father of Lies himself!

Now there is no doubt at all, that we have all to contend with a certain amount of lurking unbelief in regard to those evil spirits of which we are to think this afternoon. There *is* something strange in thinking that *we*, in this commonplace life, and living amid these familiar scenes we know, are indeed day by day subjected to the attacks and the arts of infernal spirits. It would somehow not strike us as so strange, to think of these beings as assailing human souls in distant places and in ages past. In the solitary wilderness of Sinai, amid rifted rocks and hills of red sand, it is easier to think of the Devil and his angels working upon the heart, than to think of them doing so in the case of a human being who lives in a house in an Edinburgh Row, and sometimes walks along Princes Street. Let us face these facts : little things like these have a very great practical effect on the minds of most men : and many things, not at all of the nature of argument, have a very real though undeserved influence upon our convictions and belief. And not merely is there among professing Christians a great amount of practical unbelief as regards the existence and influence of Evil Spirits : not merely are we all subjected to a strong, undefined temptation, practically to forget and set aside the solemn fact, that real persons, cleverer and sharper by far than ourselves, are ever near us, with power of mysterious access to our souls, and with the will to do us all the mischief they can : but it is doubtless known to some of you that theoretical unbelief has in some cases grown, as it very usually does, out of practical : and that many men who profess to be

Christians, have proceeded from living as if there were no malignant spirits plotting our ruin, to holding the belief that in fact there are none such. You will find men who will tell you that the existence of Satan and his angels is an antiquated doctrine, fitted for a ruder age, but not suited to our growing intelligence : they will tell you that it is not to be supposed that God would suffer such beings to exist and to assail us : and that all that was said by Christ and His Apostles with regard to evil spirits,—all that *they* said implying that there are such beings, and that they can do harm to man,—must be understood as having been said ir compliance with the vulgar way of thinking. But I think you will see that such arguments as these against the doctrine of the real being of evil spirits, are of no force whatever. As to the notion that the Almighty would not suffer such, why, there is no greater diffi- culty in understanding why He permits evil spirits, than in understanding why He permits evil men. And we know that God not only allows evil men to exist ; but allows them to tempt and mislead other human souls to evil : in short, allows them to do the self-same work which some so rashly say it is inconceivable that God should permit to be done at all. And as for the notion that Christ and the Apostles in speaking of evil spirits were merely complying with the vulgar way of thinking, —merely to put that notion plainly before our minds is enough to set it aside. See what it comes to. That there are no evil spirits : that it is a foolish error to fancy there are : that people, however, generally fancied there are : and that our Saviour, for fear of shocking their prejudice, gave in to that foolish error, and countenanced it. Now, is that conceivable? Would that have been worthy of Him who is the Truth: would that shifty, tricky, mean, uncandid policy have been like Jesus of Nazareth? No, my friends : there is no resisting the teaching of inspiration, as set forth even in those verses which form my text, that you and I, in leading our spiritual life, have to contend with real, personal beings, striving to lead us wrong : that there is something more against us than merely the force of circumstances, and the current of events in a fallen world : that not merely the evil world around us, and the evil heart within us, are driving us away from God, but that these are seconded and used by real persons of the greatest power and craft. Ought we not to seek to know something of the nature and the wiles of our great adversaries : ought we not to study with care all that God has revealed to us about them, and the ways in which they may assail us, that with His grace and blessing we may be fore-armed against their assault? Ah brethren, if any of you were told that some savage wild beast had escaped from its confinement, and was roaming the country, destroying all it met, would you not be anxious to learn where it had been seen, and how it attacked its victims, that so you might know how best to escape it? And is there less reason for fear and for caution, less reason for anxious inquiry and for careful preparation, when God's solemn word assures us, that "our adversary the Devil, as a roaring lion, walketh about, seeking whom he may devour?" We do not see him, and his subject demons: but surely, if we rightly judged, *that* does not make them less, but far more dangerous. What do you think a human robber or murderer would give for the power of rendering himself invisible at will? Would not *that* multiply a thousandfold his ability to do harm? Yes, and give those to whom he wished to do harm a thousandfold more reason to stand in hourly fear of him!

We all know that the Bible contains many references to evil spirits, unclean spirits, or devils: and it is worthy of being remembered that in the New Testament there is very much more frequent mention made of evil angels than of good angels. For whatever advantages we may ever derive from the aid and guidance of good angels, we gain by the direct intervention of God: and we are not to think of making any application to any good spirit for his help. It is not by personal applications or prayers to good angels themselves, that we can hope to get *them* for our guardians. We are not to invoke for ourselves the kindly care of those bright beings: but to ask of God to keep us and care for us by whatever instrumentality He thinks best. But it is different with evil spirits. Against *them* we are called personally to guard. We may, by our own evil thoughts and ways, tempt *them* to tempt us. The visits of pure angels have been, in the history of our race, few and far between. The great Adversary, and his accursed spirits, are ever near. To *them* we may open our hearts. For *them* we may smoothe a path to us. And *them* we may by God's grace resist, and drive away. We are exposed to great perils from *them*, against which we need to be guarded.

The teaching of Scripture, as has been said, is, that at the head of the kingdom of evil there is placed one being, of vast power, craft, and malignity. That from the earliest ages, he has been the adversary of God : and that very soon after the creation of our race, he was the tempter, too successfully, of man. " He was a murderer from the beginning :" " He is a liar, and the father of lies." " He that committeth sin is of the Devil, for the Devil sinneth from the beginning. For this purpose the Son of God was manifested, that He might destroy the works of the Devil." When the word of God, fallen upon man's heart, seems likely to grow up into good fruit there, "then cometh the Devil, and taketh away the word out of their hearts." Inferior to this great father of mischief, there is a great host of evil spirits, or demons : concerning whom we are told that they are angels who kept not their first estate, but left their own habitation : beings who having fallen into sin and misery, seek to lead others into sin and misery too. And when we find powers ascribed to Satan which somewhat perplex us, as appearing to transcend those of a mere creature ;—as when we find Scripture speaking of him as attacking and tempting many men in many places at once ;—we are to believe that he does so by means of his angels and emissaries : and so may properly be said to do what he does by them : as when we say of a military commander that he wins a battle, or occupies a province : that is, he does it through the agency of the soldiers he commands.   And thus, my friends, for what we know, there may be around us a host of evil spirits, exceeding the number of our race : invisible to our view, yet with ready access to our hearts : with craft and talent and ingenuity infinitely surpassing ours : and earnestly and ceaselessly, with the malignity of utter despair, bending those great energies upon the work of our eternal ruin.   That air may be thick with them : this church may be thronged with them : our own hearts may be in the grasp of one or of many of them ! Oh brethren, when you soberly think of all this, can there be a more appalling thought !

But the thing of practical moment for each of us, is the manner in which they make their attack upon us.   And it is not too much to say that we may be quite sure that they will attack us in the most crafty way.   And will not the most crafty way in which an evil spirit can present himself and his temptations to our mind and heart, be the way in which we least expect him to do so?   Yes : Scripture tells us that Satan can transform himself into an angel of light. He is too cunning to present himself in his own black colours, when he can veil himself in a more engaging form. We can well imagine that it might form part of the tactics of the great Adversary, to seek to induce men to believe that there are no such things as evil spirits at all : we may well trace his handiwork in that disposition to treat with levity and as a jest the mention of his ill-omened name. We can well imagine how evil spirits may set themselves to make men fancy that the mode of their attacks is widely different from what it is in fact : and so to trace their presence and influence not in evil thoughts and suggestions which weave in so naturally with the workings of our own minds, and seem to arise so spontaneously there, that it is hard to refer their origin to anything apart from ourselves ; but rather in ghastly appearances, in frightful shapes, in childish legends of compacts made in wild solitudes and written in letters of blood. Ah, brethren, not such are the assaults of Satan and the blasted beings he commands! The Devil and his angels are not so simple as to take pains to caution men against themselves. You will find people whose notion of evil spirits is of dark and awful forms, physically horrible : and the genius of the artist has often pictured on the canvas shapes so ghastly, as those in which such spirits have manifested themselves to human ken, that it might almost seem as if they fancied it likely that these malignant deceivers would take pains to announce the truth about it themselves, and bid all clearly understand how bad and foul they are. No: the day may come when they shall be revealed to all the universe, as fearful in aspect as they are evil in character: but not yet. Why, if the Devil shewed himself to our eyes or hearts in his true aspect, do you think *that* would be a temptation to any one? No: it would be the most effectual caution and warning against him. It is God's Word that tells us how he goes about like a roaring lion, seeking whom he may devour: he is not likely to announce *that* himself. Do you think a fraudulent trader would go about proclaiming that he was a rogue, and that if you dealt with him he would be sure to cheat you? If a man were trying to get you to buy his bad wares, would he be likely to take pains to tell you how bad they were? Would the cheat succeed in defrauding any one, if he laid open the arts by which he hoped to defraud men: if he openly said, Buy my knives, they won't cut: Buy my cloth, it won't wear: Embark in my ship, it is sure to go to the bottom and drown all on board? No, my friends: the evil one and his angels are not weak enough to announce to us how evil they are, and how bent upon our destruction. The old serpent did not go to the mother of our race, and say, Here is the fruit which God forbade you to eat: if you eat it you are sure to die: but never mind about *that:* it is pleasant, and just eat it notwithstanding. Nay, what were his fair words,—" Ye shall *not* surely die !" And so, brethren, when Satan would tempt us to our ruin, he is not likely formally to suggest to us, that he will give us a price in exchange for our soul: he is not likely to offer to any man possessed of reason, so much money or so much power in exchange for his eternal misery: the weakest man would hardly make a bargain like *that*, with the facts fairly stated to him: *That*, in truth, would be no temptation at all. No doubt, Satan often actually succeeds in driving a bargain which really amounts to that: no doubt he often actually gets the soul of man, and for a very poor price indeed: but man makes the bargain without seeing that he is doing so: and if the Adversary does not actually present himself in the guise of an angel of light, he does at least persuade his victim that he is not so black after all: that the sin to which he tempts is not so malignantly bad, and the doom to which he urges is doubtful and far away. It is in our own growing worldliness of spirit,—in our own heart getting more and more set upon the things of time and sense,—in our own disposition to put off the care of religion to the more convenient season which never comes,—in our own temper of careless easy-mindedness, forgetful of the awful realities of heaven and hell, and vaguely trusting that through God's mercy things will somehow go right for eternity with little thought or pains on our part,—oh brethren, it is in symptoms like *these* that we may read the fearful indications that the Devil and his angels are working too successfully upon our hearts. I do not mention the stimulus of unholy passion, of covetousness, of envy, of a Pharisaic and self-righteous spirit, of the disposition to detraction and slander: though in all these too we may read the doing of the first great slanderer of God and seducer of man. You fancy that the bitter, angry spirit that grows up within you at some slight offence, is but the working of your own natural temperament: ah, you do not know how it may be fomented and encouraged by some dark being, specially devoting himself to the task. The inquisitor of the middle ages, as he watched the rebel against priestly tyranny stretched upon the rack, fancied that it was honest religious zeal that impelled the torture which he inflicted: he little thought that while fancying he was doing God service, he was actuated by the crafty promptings of the spirit of all wrath and bitterness and cruelty within. In brief, my friends, it is reasonable and right for us to suspect the presence and influence of an evil spirit, in every temptation we ever feel to sin or error: in every intellectual process that would cast doubt upon God's revealed religion, in every impulse that would prompt to any deed or any thought that varies from the mind and example of our Blessed Saviour Himself. It is only while walking with God, in that way in which His Holy Spirit would lead us, that we can ever be sure that we are not unconsciously actuated by the direction of unclean demons: and we never can be certain, in the case of any thought **or** feeling or impulse within us, not inspired from above, that it is not whispered in our ear or instilled into our heart by some wretched and malignant fiend. Not by the mere natural working **of our** fallen mind does the evil suggestion arise : **but** **weaving in with** *that*, mysteriously co-operating with *that*, **re-inforcing** and aggravating *that*, comes the **baneful influence** from the place of perdition !

And yet, though this truth be a most awful one, **it is a** salutary **one :** it is one which it is good for **us to remember and** to reflect upon. Is there not **something here to fill** us with the greater horror and **detestation of sin : to** lead **us** to the more resolute **battling with** temptation ? **Think** that in every temptation **to sin, you have a** real being, a person, trying to **lead you into guilt and** ruin. Think that every time **you sin, you are doing** the very thing that your very **worst and most** malicious **enemy** wishes you **to do,** and is pushing and enticing **you to do !** Christian **brethren,** is not *that* a motive to hate **and** shun sin : **to** resist and battle with temptation ? **And remember, too, that by God's** grace, and by the **aid of that stronger and** mightier Spirit of holiness, **and truth, and comfort, who** is promised to be with us, **you will** not resist **in vain.** Your ally is a thousandfold more powerful than your adversary : the Spirit of the living God, who is upon your side, is able to strengthen you **to** withstand the strength, and to enlighten you to **unravel the** wiles, **even of one who, so far as we**

know, appears to be God's craftiest and mightiest, though most miserable and most wicked creature. And by the very nature of this creation which God made, honest, conscious resistance to temptation goes to make the temptation grow weaker: even as compliance with temptation goes to make the temptation grow stronger.   And the same law extends, we know, to the chief tempter of all.   How speaks God's Word? " Resist the Devil, and he will flee from you ! " Faithfully in God's strength strive against every impulse to sin : and with each successive defeat, the attacks of the father of mischief will grow weaker and less frequent.   Under that law God has bound him, that earnestly resisted he must flee : it is only where he and his agents meet a half-hearted opposition, or even find the doors of the soul thrown open to admit them, that they can enter in, and set up a sway in that heart, and bind it in chains that never will be broken,—the chains of inveterate, incradicable habit, of hopeless worldliness of soul and wickedness of life.   Oh my Christian brethren, as you care for your souls, strive and pray against temptation : you are resisting Satan then !   Every time you wilfully yield to temptation, you are welcoming the Devil and his angels to your heart : you are giving them a settlement there from which you may never be able to dislodge them, here or hereafter !   How solemn a meaning does all this cast upon that petition in our Lord's prayer, in which He bids us say, " Lead us not

into temptation, but deliver us from evil !"   Many of
you know that the word translated *evil* there, means
the evil one: so that Christ speaks of the temptation and the tempter as meaning the same thing :
"Lead us not into temptation ; but deliver us from
the tempter :" *that* is the meaning of the petition :
the prayer for deliverance from temptation is a prayer
for deliverance from Satan and his dark array.   All
temptation : everything, every influence that can ever
lead to sin or suffering, is *of* him, or *through* him, or
seconded and aided *by* him.   Oh may God's kind,
mighty Spirit, so sanctify these poor, weak, wayward
hearts. that we may rightly resist evil spirits, until they
finally flee away !

XVII.

THE NEEDFULNESS OF LOVE TO CHRIST.*

"If any man love not the Lord Jesus Christ, let him be Anathema Maranatha."—1 COR. xvi. 22.

I THINK, my friends, that words so solemn as these, need nothing beyond their own weighty meaning to commend them to our grave attention. Still, it is worth our remembering, because it is something that shews St Paul attached especial importance to them, that the great Apostle wrote them with his own hand, at the close of an Epistle which, according to his wont, he had dictated to another. Some think that it was part of "the thorn in the flesh" he bore, that his hands always trembled so, that he wrote slowly and with pain. And you can all imagine how, when this Epistle came to Corinth, and the Christians there bent over its leaves in little groups, all anxious to know what was St Paul's last message to them, though they would read with deep concern the Apostle's words, traced in the clear

* Preached at the celebration of the Sacrament of the Lord's Supper.

bold handwriting of Stephanas, and Fortunatus, and Achaicus, they would **look** with deeper interest yet, **upon** the tremulous lines, where the Apostle had at **the last taken** the pen into his own hand, and striven **to give in a** single sentence the **sum** of all he **had** said before. If there was anything in the **whole** Epistle which more than **another he** wished them **to remember,** surely they had it here !

And as to the words in which this verse **is expressed, you know** that *Anathema* means *accursed;* and *Maranatha* means *The Lord is coming.* So the text means, "**If any** man love not the Lord Jesus Christ, let him be accursed : " and it is under stood that the addition of the *Maranatha* makes a more solemn fashion of denouncing such a one's doom.

But it is easier to understand the Apostle's meaning, than it is at the first thought to approve his sentiment. It seems a curious thing, and a contradictory thing, and not like the doing of a man who knew much of human nature, to enforce, by a fearful curse, the duty of loving the kind, merciful, loving Saviour, whom we specially remember this day. For *that* is not the way to get any one to love Christ. You cannot frighten the human soul into loving. You cannot make a man love Christ, by assuring him that he shall suffer in endless perdition if he do not love Christ. Even if by such means you made any one anxious to love Christ, he might not be able to do so though he were ever so desirous. But we are to remember, that these words of St Paul are not a curse, as we understand that phrase. The text does not mean 'that' St Paul wished or desired that any one should be wretched for ever. The text only conveys that the Apostle knew that thus it *would* be; and felt that thus it ought to be. And the Apostle knew, too, that though the firmest belief that we never can be happy away from Christ, and without loving Christ, would not of itself suffice to awaken in our hearts the holy affection of love to Him; still, that it might serve a great end in making us more earnest in using all the means which directly tend to awaken that affection in our hearts. And it is in this belief, that I have selected the great principle laid down in the text, for our meditation on the morning of our Communion Sabbath. We have come here this day, especially to remember our Blessed Saviour: we have come to look upon the emblems of His broken body and shed blood, which testify His dying love towards us. We have come, hoping that the Holy Spirit of all grace, may touch our hearts with warmer than ordinary love towards Him who loved us, and gave Himself to death for us. We humbly ask it of Him, from whom all holy affections proceed, that all the solemn services of Communion may bring more plainly before us all that our Blessed Redeemer is, and all that He did and suffered for us; and so make us feel how happy it is, and how easy it is when God enables us, to love Him with heart and soul and mind. And as we know something of that love of Christ towards us, which passeth knowledge ; and (by God's grace) feel something of it within our own souls ; it will be profitable for us to see that it is no mere wilfulness on the part of the Almighty that leads Him to set up this Christian grace as of such essential and supreme importance :—that there is nothing arbitrary in the great principle, that he who does not "love the Lord Jesus Christ" never will be happy,—but that in truth he never will because he never can. I wish, my friends, to make you see the reasonableness of the great principle implied in the text : I wish to make you see the reasonableness of the service in which we engage to-day ;—that it is not merely for the pleasure of feeling warm and pure emotion that we come to the communion-table, or that we pray and seek to love our Saviour more day by day : but that in the nature of things, and by the very make of our being, it is only from love to the Saviour that our true and lasting happiness can spring ; and so, that "if any man love not the Lord Jesus Christ," he never *can* be really or lastingly happy ! Waiting at the holy table : waiting for the breathing of the Blessed Spirit upon our hearts : praying for clearer views of our Redeemer's love towards us, and for warmer love towards Him ; we are enjoying no mere transient privilege : we are laying the foundations of our eternal bliss : we are sowing the seed of which we may hope to reap everlasting life and never-ending happiness !

We can discern two reasons why we can be truly and endlessly happy only if we give the Saviour the first place in our hearts: two reasons why "if any man love not the Lord Jesus Christ," he must be for ever unsatisfied, and unhappy, and all that is meant by the words Anathema Maranatha. One of these reasons arises out of the essential nature of the gospel scheme of salvation : the other reason arises out of the essential nature of the Christian Heaven, and of the happiness provided there.

And so, in the first place, let us think what is the way of salvation which is set before us in the gospel : what is the sum of all the duty the gospel requires of us : what is the inward spring in our hearts, from which all our Christian duties are to flow, and from which our entire Christian character is to be developed? What is the essence of Christianity in the heart? Do you not know, my friends, that it is just love to Christ? You all know what it is we must do to be saved: "Believe in the Lord Jesus Christ, and thou shalt be saved," said St Paul at Philippi : and what is meant by believing in Christ, but just going with trusting and loving hearts, and committing to His love and power ourselves, our souls, and all that concerns us for time or eternity? Love to the Saviour is of the very essence of saving faith. We cannot truly and savingly believe, till we are enabled entirely to trust God's love to us, to be sure that He loves us, and gave His Son to die for us because He loved us, and wished to see us happy and holy for ever; and till thus we are enabled to feel something of reciprocated love towards Him who "first loved us." You remember what was the first and great commandment, even in the sterner days of the Law,—even before God manifested Himself in the gracious face of Christ,—even through ages in which men were ever being reminded, that "the soul that sinneth it shall die," and that "cursed is every one that continueth not in all things written in the Law to do them." Even in those days, we know, from the highest of all authority, that the commandment which grasped the Law's whole spirit and essence, was, "Thou shalt love the Lord thy God with heart and soul and strength and mind." *This* was "the first and great commandment" even then :—even when the manifestation of God that came readiest to men's recollection was in the flames and thunders of Sinai. But how much more now, in these days of Gospel light, in which God has revealed Himself to us through our Saviour, and told us that *He* is the image of the invisible God : now, when in our desires to know what God is, we have but to picture to ourselves that Blessed Redeemer, who went about doing good : now, when we have but to look to Jesus, and think that in looking at Him, we see God,—that in Him. the kind, patient, merciful, considerate

Saviour, who did so much for us, and suffered so infinitely for us, we see God! Yes, it is at once the way to salvation, and the sum of Christian duty, to "love the Lord Jesus Christ:" and what wonder, then, if the apostle tells us, that the man who turns his back upon the only way of salvation, and refuses to admit to his heart the one motive that will prompt to everything right, must be excluded from the enjoyment of the blessings which the Saviour died to purchase for us? To trust God, as seen in the face of His Son; and to believe that He loves us,—*that* is faith: *that* is what we must do to be saved. And to love God, as seen in the face of His Son; and to seek to testify our love by our whole life,—*that* is Christian duty: *that* is all we have to do. And thus you will see how fixed and unalterable is the solemn principle implied in the words of the text, when you consider that to refuse to love Christ,—to refuse to seek that Spirit, never denied to the earnest seeker, who will enable us to love Christ,—is to refuse salvation in the only way in which it is possible we can receive it. "If any man love not the Lord Jesus Christ," he *must* be eternally lost; because that man wilfully and obstinately refuses to be saved!

No: it was not mere wilfulness in St Paul that led him to write this text. He was not seeking to set out some crotchet of his own; nor giving to the affection of love towards the Redeemer an importance beyond what would have been accorded to it by other inspired writers.   He meant that here was a test that went to the root of the matter : he meant that everything was wrong in that man's condition for eternity, who was not seeking daily for more love to Christ.   For the fact that a man has it not, is proof that he does not want it : for to desire it and to pray for it is to get it. This affection of love to Christ is one of the very first of the "fruits of the Spirit ;" and you all remember how fully and unreservedly that Spirit is promised to all who sincerely wish and ask for Him.   No one, we may be sure, who honestly wishes to love the Saviour, will find it a hard task to do so.   And when the great Apostle wrote this awful warning in the text, it was as if he had said to a poisoned man, Here is the remedy, here is the antidote ; but if you refuse to take it, you will die !   It was as if he had said to a drowning man, Here is a branch, catch it and hold it ; for if you do not, you will go down.   It was indeed saying to the poor, lost sinner, Here is the one way to safety, oh hasten to pursue it : Here are peace and pardon of- fered to you and urged upon you,—oh lay hold of them and embrace them : but if you will not, then your blood be upon your own head !

But now in the second place, we come to the other reason which is to be suggested why " if any man love not the Lord Jesus Christ," he never shall be satisfied and happy.   It is this : that by the very nature of the Christian Heaven, and by the very nature of the human soul, it is impossible that any man should be happy eternally unless he loves the Saviour.

Here, my friends, is a great practical truth, which cannot be too deeply impressed upon us. Some may be inclined to think that it is hard in God, and not like His infinite love that gave His Son for us, and not like His own declaration that He is " not willing that any should perish,"—to condemn any human soul to final woe. Might He not, at the close of any life, however sinful, in this world, pardon the poor soul's sins, and suffer it to find some lowly place in the better country? But what, if *that* be impossible? What if it be so, that even apart from any question as to how this might concern God's justice and truth,— what if it be so, that Heaven would be no place of happiness except to souls redeemed and renewed and sanctified? And thus it is, of a surety. In the very nature of things, a human being cannot be happy eternally unless he love the Saviour.

We all know that there is but one Place where we can be perfectly happy. It is agreed on all hands that *this* life never can be evenly joyous,—that there always will be some alloy, some vexation,—a sepulchre in the garden, a shadow in the home. The mere uncertainty that hangs over this life,—the knowledge that a single day's chances may take from us all we hold dear,—even *that* would suffice to shew that this can never be our rest. It is only in Heaven that we shall be right ;—shall be holy, happy, and *safe*. But then, what kind of place is heaven? What is the essential thing about heaven? Not the outward beauty: not the golden thrones, the sapphire pavements, nor the glassy sea: not the matchless music, nor the triumphal palms, nor the spotless robes, nor the day without night: No, the great thing there is the constant presence of the Saviour. The great thing there, we know from the same Apostle who wrote our text, is that *there* the soul " shall be for ever with the Lord." And here, you see, is the essential point of difference between the Christian Heaven, and the Paradises promised by false prophets and false religions. *They* have always been described as places which would make any one happy, who could only find entrance into them, and find a home in them. You can see in all accounts of them, that first belief of man,—that belief of a primitive age and an untutored race, that happiness is a matter of one's outward lot. That belief is deep set in human nature. You remember the great moralist's account of the Happy Valley, where every one was sure to be blest. The popular belief that there might be a scene so fair that it would make happy any human being who should be allowed to dwell in it, is strongly shewn in the name universally given to the spot which was inhabited by the parents of our race before evil was known. It was the *Garden of Delight*: and the name describes not the beauty of the scene alone, but the effect it would produce upon the mind of its tenants. The paradises of all rude nations are places which profess to make every one happy who enters them, quite apart from any consideration of the world which he might bear within his own breast. And the same principle, that the outward scene and circumstances in which a human being is placed, are able to make him perfectly and unfailingly happy, whatever he himself may be, is taken for granted in all we are told of the Paradise of the Moslem, of the Scandinavian Valhalla, the Amenti of the old Egyptian, the Peruvian's Spirit-world, and the Red Man's Land of Souls. But all we are told of the Christian Heaven, founds upon a far deeper and farther-reaching view. It goes upon *this*, that happiness is something within the breast: that it is the happy soul within, rather than the beautiful scenes without, that shall make man happy. The Christian heaven, with far deeper truth, is less a locality than a character: its happiness is a relation between the employments provided, and the spiritual condition of those who engage in them. And it was a grand and noble thing, when a creed came forth, which utterly repudiated the notion of a Fortunate Island, into which, after any life you liked, you had but to smuggle yourself, and all was well. It was a grand thing, and an intensely practical thing, to point to an unseen world, which will make happy the man who is prepared for it, and who is fit for it; and no one else.

I do not mean by this, that Heaven is not a real,

substantial place: as real and substantial as this world. It is all that, no doubt: the great doctrine of the Resurrection of the Body implies a solid, material country: we "seek a country" not of mists and shadows, but one which material feet can tread, and hands of flesh and blood can grasp. But still remember, that the great thing about heaven is, that Christ is *there:* that *there* "we shall be for ever with the Lord." And now, my friends, do you not see how impossible it is that any one should be happy in heaven, unless he loves the Saviour? It would not make any one happy to be with Christ, unless he loves Christ: it would not make you happy to be with one you did not care for. You see how true the text is ; and why the text is true. Heaven is the only place where man can be happy : a man without love to Christ would not be happy in heaven : and therefore, a man without love to Christ would not be happy anywhere. He must, anywhere in God's creation be unsatisfied, restless, wretched : all that is conveyed by that terrible *Anathema Maranatha.*

Oh, brethren, let us bear this in our memory: and let us pray this day at the Holy Table for more love to Christ ! Praying for that, and getting that, as we shall if we pray for it, we are making ourselves such that we shall be happy in heaven. Wanting that love, we should not care for heaven, even if we got there. It is our common way to picture heaven to ourselves as an extraordinarily beautiful place. A great many people think of heaven just as something differing in degree from this world, but not differing in kind :—just as an incomparably finer and more beautiful world, but the same *sort* of thing. They think that all that is most beauteous here, is imaged there in happier beauty: they think of brighter skies, and calmer seas,—of "an ampler ether, a diviner air :" of streams that run in living light; of walls of gems and gates of pearl, and light that never fades and songs that never cease : they dwell upon all that august and splendid materialism of the better world, which is piled up, like sunset clouds, in the closing chapters of the Revelation : they cherish a thought,—do not some of you here cherish a thought,—that this outward glory is the thing that *makes* heaven ;—that the first thought of the blest soul entering there will be, what a magnificent and beautiful place its eternal home is ; —that heaven is just, in all the literalness of the words, "another and a better *world!*" Oh, you mistake it, if you dream of such a thought as this ! It is not mere external loveliness that will make the Paradise of the Christian's strivings and the Christian's hopes. No : beautiful as heaven may be : beautiful as heaven must be : it would be a poor and empty thing to make the immortal soul's eternal bliss, if you had said your best of it when you had told us of its outward beauty. It is not walls of gems and gates of pearl that will make the soul happy! It must be something that eye hath not seen and ear hath not heard that shall do *that!* And we know what it is: it is the presence, the society, the constant love of Christ. It is that there "we shall be for ever with the Lord!" It is that there "we shall be like Him, for we shall see Him as He is!" The power of heaven to make completely happy, lies in this,—that our Redeemer is there!

Nor is there anything mystical or irrational in all this. Even in this world, it makes us happy to be with those we love. You have all known what it is to feel happy by being in the society of those you love: you have perhaps thought that though you were carried away to almost any corner of this world, you would still be happy and content if those you love were still around you there. And the great happiness of heaven will just be a perfect degree of that same thing of which an imperfect degree, amid many clogs and drawbacks, made the great happiness here. And the deeper and the more pervading the believer's love to his Saviour, the greater will be his happiness in heaven. The thought which should ever come warmest home to the Christian's heart, as he looks onward to the Golden City, is that his Redeemer will always be there. *That* is what makes heaven. All the glories and beauties of the Revelation, are mere slight incidental trifles, when compared with *that!* There may be pearly streams and silver sand,—we do not know: there may be diamond dews glittering on fadeless flowers: there may be golden pavements and glassy seas: there may be palms of triumph, and thrones of gold, and palaces not built with hands, that tower into that sky of cloudless blue: it may be that every description the Bible gives us of the materialism of heaven shall be fulfilled to the letter: but oh! the grand thing there will be the Beatific Presence of Christ: to look on His kind face, to hear His kind voice: to know that *that* is the very Redeemer that died for us, the very Jesus of Nazareth who went about doing good: the God who was with us, and kept us in all ways that we went, and guided our wandering footsteps through the perplexing paths of life; and spread His covering wings around us till our wanderings closed, and our souls arrived in peace at our Father's house for ever!

And what shall we say to all this, for a comment upon our text? "If any man love not the Lord Jesus Christ, he shall be Anathema Maranatha." You see why it must be so. If we be such that Heaven would not make us happy, then happy we can never be. If any human being will not love Christ, then there is no provision in the universe for making him happy. It is no arbitrary appointment that the soul which will not love Jesus should be wretched for ever: it is the necessary consequence of its wanting that pure, pervading love: and apart from the positive woes of perdition, an eternity of wretchedness grows from the want of love to Christ, as naturally as the oak grows from the acorn, or the harvest from the scattered grain. It is not that love to Christ merits heaven: it does far better, it *makes* heaven! Carry the soul that loves the Saviour supremely into His presence for ever: and it is in heaven! But remember, it is only the presence of those he deeply loves, that can make a human being happy. It would not make us happy to be always with one we did not care for. And so, in order to taste, and appreciate, and enjoy, the happiness of the Christian heaven, we must love Christ supremely. It is only *then* that heaven can make us happy. If you do not love Him, then *your* souls could no more feel heaven's blessedness, though you were placed in the midst of it, than the blind man's eyes can discern the summer day, that spreads around him in its golden light! The love of Christ is as it were the organ of sensation that takes note of heaven's blessedness: and every soul that feels nothing of that love need not dream that the mere fact of being excluded from Heaven adds one grain to the burden of its dreary wretchedness. Place such a soul in the very midst of heaven,—where the atmosphere of the Redeemer's presence is diffused like fragrance in the spring-tide air;—and still that flood of bliss that wakens ever-fresh delight in the redeemed man's soul, would fall as effectless and as unnoted upon that unchanged spirit, as the bursts of angelic melody upon the ear to which all sound is silence, or as the sunbeams of June's blue sky upon the eye to which all light is dark! So true, so inevitable, is the solemn principle of the text, that "if any man love not the Lord Jesus Christ, he must be Anathema Maranatha!"

And thus you see, Christian friends, that in coming to this holy place to-day, to celebrate a rite which is especially fitted to awaken in us warmer love to our kind Redeemer; we have not come merely that we might enjoy something of kindly and pleasant emotion. It *is* painful to hate, and it *is* pleasant to love: but we do not now seek to love our Saviour merely because it is pleasant. It is the thing in us, *that* love of Him who loved us and died for us, from which all our future bliss, by the nature of things, must flow. And it might be a hard saying, that we never can be happy if we do not love Christ, if the love of Christ were a difficult thing to get, or a painful thing to feel. But who shall complain of this text, stern as at the first glance it seems, when we think that it requires of us nothing more, than that we should open our hearts to a pure affection which will make our hearts happier than they ever were before:—a pure affection which the Blessed Spirit is willing and waiting to work in us, if we do but sincerely desire to possess it! Love Christ, and then all will be well: well for our soul's salvation, well for our daily duty, well for our comfort and peace so long as God shall spare us here. Surely it is not difficult to love Him! Think how good and kind He was and is: think of what He did for us: think of the precious death and of the unutterable agony, undergone for us, which we specially com- memorate this day! If you have ever seen something that warmed and touched your heart, in a mother's self-sacrificing love for her child, as she watched that little thing through days and nights of suffering that threatened to end its short life: think that in all that tender care you had given you the faintest and farthest shadow of that unwearying love that dwells in our kind Redeemer's heart. And though you may shrink from absolute God, clad in those incomprehensible perfections: though you cannot give your love to infinite space and infinite years: yet surely you do not shrink away from Jesus of Nazareth: surely you could have loved *Him* in His days in this world: surely you can love Him yet! What hearts should we have if we did not love Him! How infinitely did He surpass all human excellence; all that ever you loved in human being: how much He did, how infinitely He suffered, for you! You would not have been afraid to see that gracious face looking upon you: you would not have been afraid to touch the hem of His garment: you would have gone to Him confidently as a little child to a kind mother: you would have feared no repulse, no impatience, as you told out to Him the story of all your sins, and wants, and cares ! Oh that we might understand something of His undying love towards us ; and that by the meditations of a Communion season, we may feel our souls, and all that is within us stirred up to deeper and purer love towards Him !

THE END.

Printed by Ballantyne & Company, Edinburgh.

www.ingramcontent.com/pod-product-compliance
Lightning Source LLC
Chambersburg PA
CBHW031030120726
47905CB00007B/2122